EYEWITNESS
FISH

European
John Dory

Gurnard

Pike skull

One-spot
yellow wrasse

Seahorse

Scorpion fish

Cuban hogfish

EYEWITNESS
FISH

Fairy basslet

Written by
STEVE PARKER

Triggerfish

Catfish

Thornback
ray

Yellow boxfish

Yellow cichlid

Atlantic
blue tang

DK

DK | Penguin Random House

REVISED EDITION

DK DELHI
Senior Editor Rupa Rao
Senior Art Editor Vikas Chauhan
Art Editors Noopur Dalal, Aparajita Sen
Assistant Art Editor Anastasia Baliyan
DTP Designers Pawan Kumar, Rakesh Kumar, Vikram Singh
Picture Researcher Vishal Ghavri
Managing Editor Kingshuk Ghoshal
Managing Art Editor Govind Mittal
Jacket Designer Juhi Sheth
Senior Jackets Coordinator Priyanka Sharma Saddi

DK LONDON
Editor Kelsie Besaw   **Art Editor** Chrissy Barnard
Senior US Editor Megan Douglass
US Executive Editor Lori Cates Hand
Managing Editor Francesca Baines
Managing Art Editor Philip Letsu
Production Editor Jacqueline Street-Elkayam
Senior Production Controller Jude Crozier
Jacket Design Development Manager Sophia MTT
Publisher Andrew Macintyre
Associate Publishing Director Liz Wheeler
Art Director Karen Self
Publishing Director Jonathan Metcalf

Consultant Helen Scales

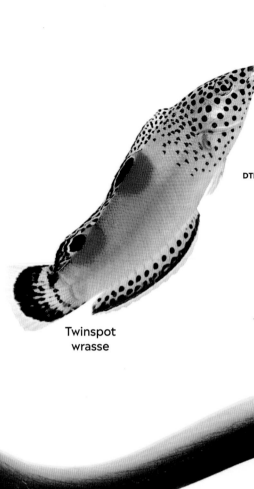

Twinspot
wrasse

Banded
pipefish

Ribbon
eel

Birdnosed
wrasse

FIRST EDITION

DK LONDON
Project Editor Susan McKeever   **Art Editor** Neville Graham
Senior Editor Sophie Mitchell   **Senior Art Editor** Julia Harris
Editorial Director Sue Unstead   **Art Director** Anne-Marie Bulat
Special Photography Dave King, Kim Taylor, Jane Burton, and Colin Keates
Editorial Consultant Gordon Howes, the Natural History Museum, London

This Eyewitness Guide® has been conceived by
Dorling Kindersley Limited and Editions Gallimard.

This American Edition, 2022
First American Edition, 1988
Published in the United States by DK Publishing
1745 Broadway, 20th Floor, New York, NY 10019

A catalog record for this book
is available from the Library of Congress.
ISBN 978-0-7440-6252-6 (Paperback)
ISBN 978-0-7440-6253-3 (ALB)

DK books are available at special discounts when purchased
in bulk for sales promotions, premiums, fund-raising, or
educational use. For details, contact: DK Publishing Special Markets,
1745 Broadway, 20th Floor, New York, NY 10019
SpecialSales@dk.com

Printed and bound in China

Underside of
gurnard

For the curious
www.dk.com

MIX
Paper | Supporting
responsible forestry
FSC C018179

This book was made with Forest Stewardship
Council™ certified paper—one small step in
DK's commitment to a sustainable future.
For more information go to
www.dk.com/our-green-pledge

Contents

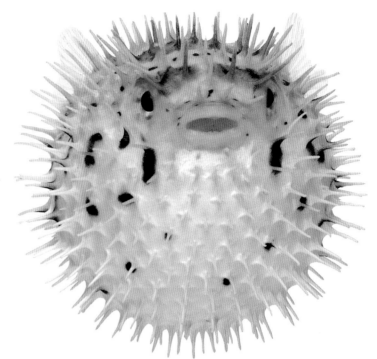

Fully inflated porcupine fish

What is a fish?

From brightly colored tropical fish to sleek, streamlined sharks, fish are a vast and varied group of aquatic creatures. There are three main groups of fish—bony, cartilaginous, and jawless (p.9). Although each group is very different, they have a number of features in common. Most fish live in water, breathe with their gills, have scales, and swim using their fins. All fish are vertebrates, which means that they have a backbone, and an internal skeleton rather than an outside "shell," or exoskeleton.

Mermaid tales
Across cultures, many stories have been told of merpeople who are part human, part fish. Sailors on long voyages may have mistaken some sea mammals for mermaids.

Fish features
The European carp (right) has typical fish features. Fish generally have a streamlined shape, which allows them to slip smoothly through the water. Most fish have several fins to help them steer, including a dorsal fin, an anal fin, paired pectoral and pelvic fins on each side of the body, and the caudal fin, or tail.

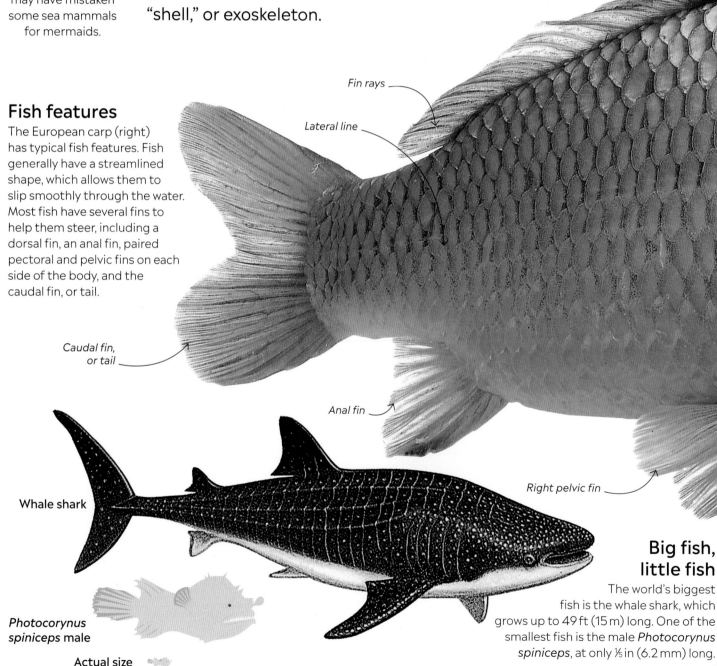

Fin rays

Lateral line

Caudal fin, or tail

Anal fin

Right pelvic fin

Whale shark

Photocorynus spiniceps male

Actual size

Big fish, little fish
The world's biggest fish is the whale shark, which grows up to 49 ft (15 m) long. One of the smallest fish is the male *Photocorynus spiniceps*, at only ⅕ in (6.2 mm) long.

What is not a fish?

Some animals are mistakenly thought of as "fish" simply because they live in water. Fish-shaped dolphins are mammals, starfish are echinoderms, and shellfish, like cuttlefish, are in fact mollusks.

Atlantic cuttlefish

Bottlenose dolphin

Dorsal fin

Overlapping scales

FEELING IN WATER

Fish sense vibrations in the water using their lateral line—a fluid-filled canal that runs along each side of the body. The vibrations shake tiny lumps of jelly in the canal. Hairs in the jelly turn the vibrations into nerve messages that are then sent to the brain.

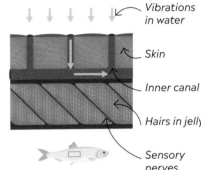

Vibrations in water

Skin

Inner canal

Hairs in jelly

Sensory nerves to brain

Eye

Nostril

Horny lips

Mouth

Belly

Right pectoral fin

Leaping salmon making the journey from sea to river

👁 EYEWITNESS

Jean-Bernard Caron
French-Canadian paleontologist Jean-Bernard Caron (right) and British paleontologist Simon Conway Morris discovered fossils of the oldest-known fish, *Metaspriggina walcotti*. It lived 518 million years ago, had protruding eyes, and breathed through seven pairs of gills.

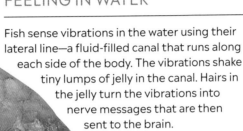

Fresh or salt?

Most fish can only live in either fresh water or salt water. A few, such as the salmon, leave the sea to swim up rivers and breed in fresh water, while others, such as eels, swim from rivers and lakes back out to sea to spawn.

Inside a **fish**

The internal organs of fish are similar to those of other animals, but they have gills for absorbing oxygen rather than lungs. The skeleton provides a framework for the body, and the brain receives information using sense organs such as the eyes and lateral line (p.7). Many bony fish have a gas-filled swim bladder that inflates or deflates, allowing the fish to move up and down in the water.

HOW FISH BREATHE

A fish "breathes" by drawing water containing dissolved oxygen into its mouth and pumping it over its gills. The oxygen passes through the gill membranes and into the fish's blood to be distributed around the body. Inside the gill chambers, there is a fairly constant flow of water. When the fish takes in a mouthful of water, the flap-like gill cover (operculum) shuts tight. The fish closes its mouth, forcing the water to flow past the gills and exit through the gill slits.

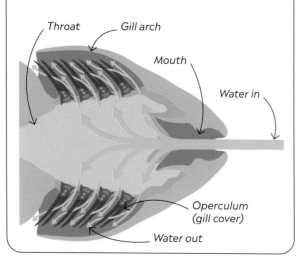

Throat

Gill arch

Mouth

Water in

Operculum (gill cover)

Water out

Multipurpose gills
Many fish, such as this striped mackerel, use their gills not just to breathe but also to eat. As the mackerel swims with its mouth open, water passes over gill rakers, which catch food particles, like a sieve, for the fish to swallow.

Throat

Gill arches support the gill filaments and gill rakers.

Gill filaments are folded structures with a huge surface area for absorbing oxygen.

Gill rakers are stiff, comblike structures that filter small food, such as zooplankton, from the water.

Bony fish
can weigh from as little as 3½ oz (0.001 g) to 2 tons.

Main fish groups

Over time, thousands of fish species have become extinct. Early fossils give clues as to how modern species are related (p.12). Some species are in groups on their own as they are the only living relatives of extinct species.

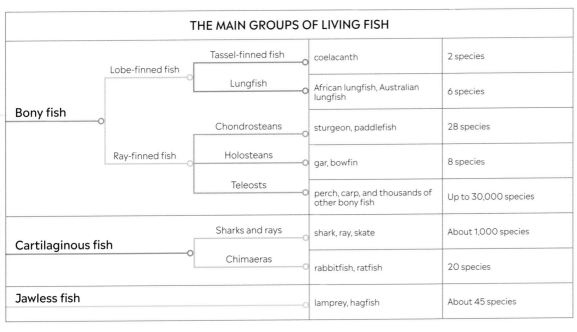

THE MAIN GROUPS OF LIVING FISH				
Bony fish	Lobe-finned fish	Tassel-finned fish	coelacanth	2 species
		Lungfish	African lungfish, Australian lungfish	6 species
	Ray-finned fish	Chondrosteans	sturgeon, paddlefish	28 species
		Holosteans	gar, bowfin	8 species
		Teleosts	perch, carp, and thousands of other bony fish	Up to 30,000 species
Cartilaginous fish	Sharks and rays		shark, ray, skate	About 1,000 species
	Chimaeras		rabbitfish, ratfish	20 species
Jawless fish			lamprey, hagfish	About 45 species

Bony fish

The internal organs of most bony fish are found in the lower half of the body. The rest of the body consists of muscles used for swimming.

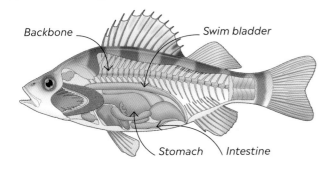

Backbone · Swim bladder · Stomach · Intestine

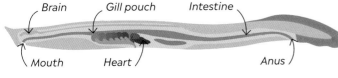

Brain · Gill pouch · Intestine · Mouth · Heart · Anus

Cartilaginous fish

A shark has similar internal organs to a bony fish, but no swim bladder. The intestine has a spiral valve which absorbs nutrients.

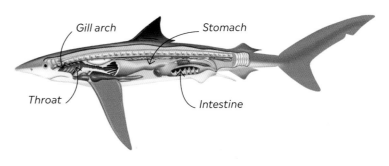

Gill arch · Stomach · Throat · Intestine

Jawless fish

The hagfish's digestive system is little more than a straight tube. The fish breathes through gill pouches, lined with blood vessels.

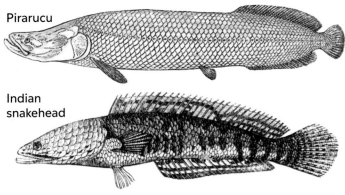

Pirarucu

Indian snakehead

Breathing out of water

Some fish breathe by gulping air and absorbing its oxygen. The pirarucu gulps air into a swim bladder linked to its throat, while the Indian snakehead takes air into folded pouches lined with blood vessels.

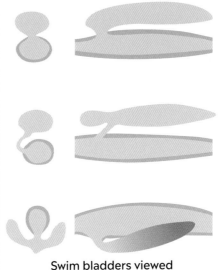

Swim bladders viewed from front and side

Adaptable swim bladder

Most bony fish have a swim bladder (top) to control buoyancy. In some tropical freshwater fish, it is attached to the hearing organs (middle). Lungfish have two swim bladders that absorb oxygen from swallowed air (bottom).

The bones of a **fish**

Most fish have skeletons made of bone. The skeleton has three main regions: the skull, which houses the brain; the backbone, which holds the spine and ribs; and the "fin skeleton"—the bones that support the fins and tail. Sharks and rays have skeletons made of cartilage instead of bone and are called cartilaginous fish. Some fish, such as sturgeon, have skeletons made of both cartilage and bone.

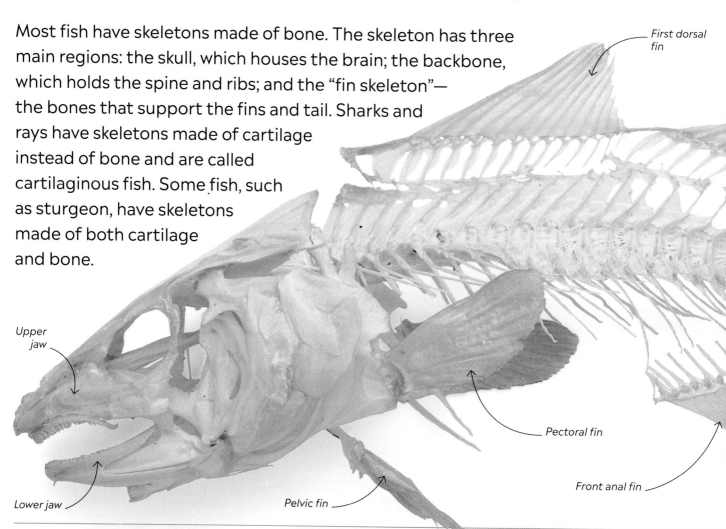

First dorsal fin

Upper jaw

Lower jaw

Pelvic fin

Pectoral fin

Front anal fin

A load of old bones

Over time, fish skeletons evolved to cope with different lifestyles. Some areas became bigger, while others shrunk to almost nothing when they were no longer needed. Some unusual parts of skeletons are shown to the right.

Stout, not speedy
The cascadura's backbone is stout and inflexible.

Trunkfish
The trunkfish's backbone has long rods that support the dorsal fin. Its body is covered with bony, six-sided scales, which work as a protective armor for the fish.

Trunkfish

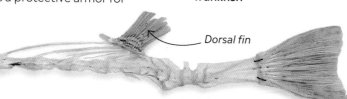

Dorsal fin

Centrum, strengthened by fibers

Basker's backbone
The basking shark has a cartilage skeleton. This is the centrum (central portion) of one of the vertebrae that make up its backbone.

The fish's framework

This skeleton of an Atlantic cod is typical of most "true" bony fish. There are two main types of fish bone. Cartilage bones form their shapes in cartilage (a tough, elastic tissue), then change into bone as the fish matures. Dermal bones develop from layers in the skin.

Atlantic cod

An Atlantic cod can weigh up to
220 lb
(100 kg).

Second dorsal fin

Spine

Fin rays

Rear anal fin

Tail vertebrae

Caudal fin (tail)

Ever-green bones

Marine garfishes are often caught by people who fish. But people are put off from eating marine garfish because of the strange bright-green color of its skeleton—the color lasts even after boiling.

Fishy "arthritis"

Spadefish often develop a disease that causes swellings on the bones and fin rays (right). This may be caused by a buildup of minerals such as calcium.

Curved centrum

In most bony fish, the centrum is concave (like a dish). But in the freshwater gar, it is convex (domed).

Convex centrum of freshwater gar

Concave centrum of pike

Vertebrae showing bone disease

Open-ocean sailor

This vertebra (below) is from a sailfish—one of the fastest swimmers in the sea. Large ridges anchor the muscles and stabilize the fish as it swims.

Sailfish

Large projecting ridges

Sailfish vertebra

Tail vertebrae of a trunkfish

Early fish

The first fish appeared in the seas almost 500 million years ago. Fossils show that, unlike most modern fish, early fish had no jaws, fins, or scales. However, they did have a kind of flexible backbone, which anchored powerful muscles to propel the creature along. As primitive fish evolved, they developed jaws (around 435 million years ago) that allowed them to bite and chew. Today, all fish except the lampreys and hagfish have jaws of some kind.

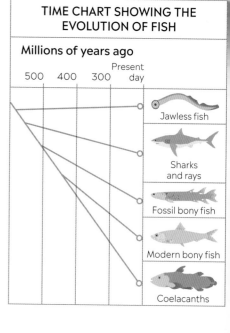

TIME CHART SHOWING THE EVOLUTION OF FISH

Millions of years ago

500	400	300	Present day

Jawless fish

Sharks and rays

Fossil bony fish

Modern bony fish

Coelacanths

A bony shield protected the fish.

Restoration of Cephalaspis

Jawless wonder

This *Cephalaspis* fossil is nearly 400 million years old. Most early fish like these had round, fleshy mouths for sucking instead of jaws.

Famous fish

In 1938, scientists were startled by the discovery of a coelacanth in South Africa—it was thought that these creatures had died out 80 million years ago. However, it appeared that local people had been catching them for years and had even been using their scales as a form of sandpaper!

There are only two living species of coelacanths but more than
100 fossil species.

Restoration of Palaeoniscus

First of the ray-fins

The palaeonisciformes were the first bony, ray-finned fish. At first, the fin rays lay parallel to the body, but gradually they splayed out like those of most modern fish. This *Palaeoniscus* fossil dates back 250 million years.

Individual body scales are clearly visible.

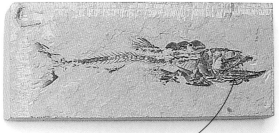

The teleosts
Eurypholis is a teleost, or "true" bony fish (p.9) that lived between 200 to 100 million years ago. It has the streamlined shape and sharp teeth of a hunter.

Large predatory mouth

Rounded holostean
Dapedium belonged to the holostean group that were common 190 million years ago. Holosteans had a fully developed backbone, but the rest of the skeleton was poorly developed.

This *Eusthenopteron* fossil shows the bones of the head and skeleton.

Fins to legs
Around 385 million years ago *Eusthenopteron* had powerful pectoral and pelvic fins, which led people to think it crawled onto land. In fact, it was their descendants, such as *Acanthostega*, which evolved legs around 365 million years ago, while they were still living mostly in water. They then gave rise to all the land-living vertebrates.

Restoration of *Eusthenopteron*

Almost there
With their flexible fins and lightweight scales, teleost fish, such as *Stichocentrus* (left), gradually took over from many of the early fish groups.

Ray wings
Heliobatis (right) is a kind of stingray. Modern rays are very similar to those that lived millions of years ago.

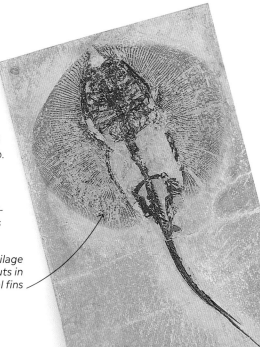

Flipper-like fins

Cartilage struts in pectoral fins

Scale story

Most fish are covered with a layer of overlapping, transparent plates called scales. There are four main types of fish scales. Cycloid scales, found on salmon and carp, have a smooth surface. Ctenoid scales, seen on bass and perch, have tiny teeth along the edge, like combs. Ganoid scales, found on garfish, are hard and diamond-shaped. Sharks and most rays have placoid scales, also called denticles, which look like tiny teeth embedded in the skin.

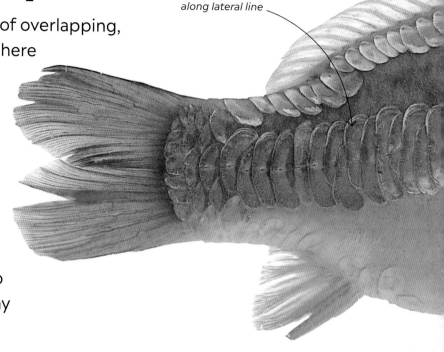

Large scales along lateral line

Sturgeon

Sturgeon scute

Sturgeon's scutes

Sturgeons have five rows of large, flat scutes (bony plates) along the body. A scute can be up to 4 in (10 cm) wide.

Sturgeon skin showing three rows of scutes

Diamond-shaped interlocking scales

Side view of garfish scales

Nonslip grip

People once used sharkskin as a grip for swords. Shark and ray scales are generally tooth-shaped and have a sandpaper-like texture.

Chain-mail scales

The North American garfish has close-fitting ganoid scales that provide tough armor. Early settlers used garfish skin to cover their plows.

Garfish

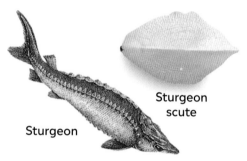

Shark scales as seen under a microscope

Coelacanth scale

The coelacanth has different scales from other fish. Each scale is a bony plate with small toothlike spines.

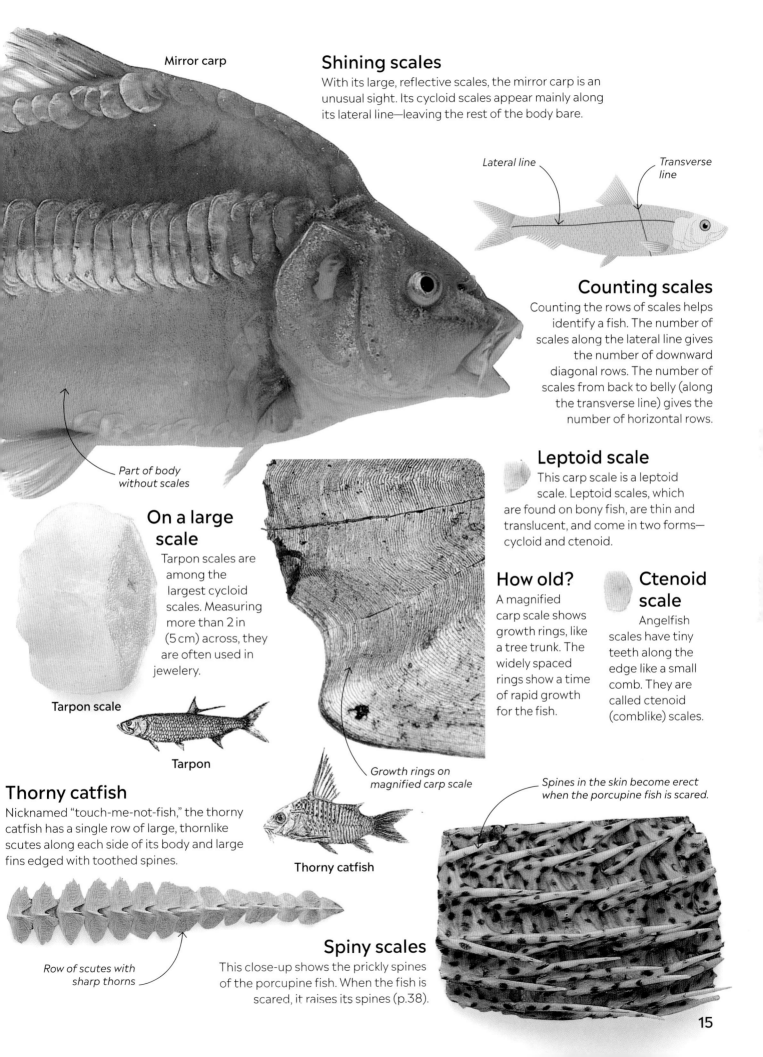

Shining scales

With its large, reflective scales, the mirror carp is an unusual sight. Its cycloid scales appear mainly along its lateral line—leaving the rest of the body bare.

Mirror carp

Part of body without scales

Lateral line

Transverse line

Counting scales

Counting the rows of scales helps identify a fish. The number of scales along the lateral line gives the number of downward diagonal rows. The number of scales from back to belly (along the transverse line) gives the number of horizontal rows.

Leptoid scale

This carp scale is a leptoid scale. Leptoid scales, which are found on bony fish, are thin and translucent, and come in two forms—cycloid and ctenoid.

On a large scale

Tarpon scales are among the largest cycloid scales. Measuring more than 2 in (5 cm) across, they are often used in jewelery.

Tarpon scale

Tarpon

How old?

A magnified carp scale shows growth rings, like a tree trunk. The widely spaced rings show a time of rapid growth for the fish.

Ctenoid scale

Angelfish scales have tiny teeth along the edge like a small comb. They are called ctenoid (comblike) scales.

Growth rings on magnified carp scale

Thorny catfish

Nicknamed "touch-me-not-fish," the thorny catfish has a single row of large, thornlike scutes along each side of its body and large fins edged with toothed spines.

Thorny catfish

Spines in the skin become erect when the porcupine fish is scared.

Row of scutes with sharp thorns

Spiny scales

This close-up shows the prickly spines of the porcupine fish. When the fish is scared, it raises its spines (p.38).

15

A riot of color

Fish come in an amazing variety of colors and patterns. Color can camouflage a fish from both predators and prey—silvery greens and blues camouflage some species in open water, while brilliant reds, yellows, and blues conceal others among coral reefs. Spots, stripes, and patches can also help confuse predators by breaking up (disrupting) a fish's shape.

Pearl-scaled butterfly fish

Pearly scales
In the pearl-scaled butterfly fish, the yellow and orange colors typical of butterfly fish only appear at the tail end.

Dark stripes
The clown loach hides on lake-beds, where its broad, dark stripes look like plant stems.

Clown loach

Barbels

False eyespot

Tails you lose
The forceps fish has a false eyespot by its tail. As a predator moves to attack the "head," the fish swishes its fins and darts off the other way.

Forceps fish

Long mouth for nibbling in crevices

False eyespot on dorsal fin to distract predators

Eye hidden by stripe

Zebra in the grass
To hide from predators, this banded pipefish lies horizontally—looking like 28 stems!

Fairy basslet
Regal purple
The bright hues of the fairy basslet are clearly seen by intruders.

Eye surprise
Flicking up its dorsal fin, the one-spot yellow wrasse surprises predators with its dark eye-spot.

Dark spot on dorsal fin

Growing colors
As the French angelfish grows, its off-white bars turn a vivid yellow.

French angelfish

Transparent tail

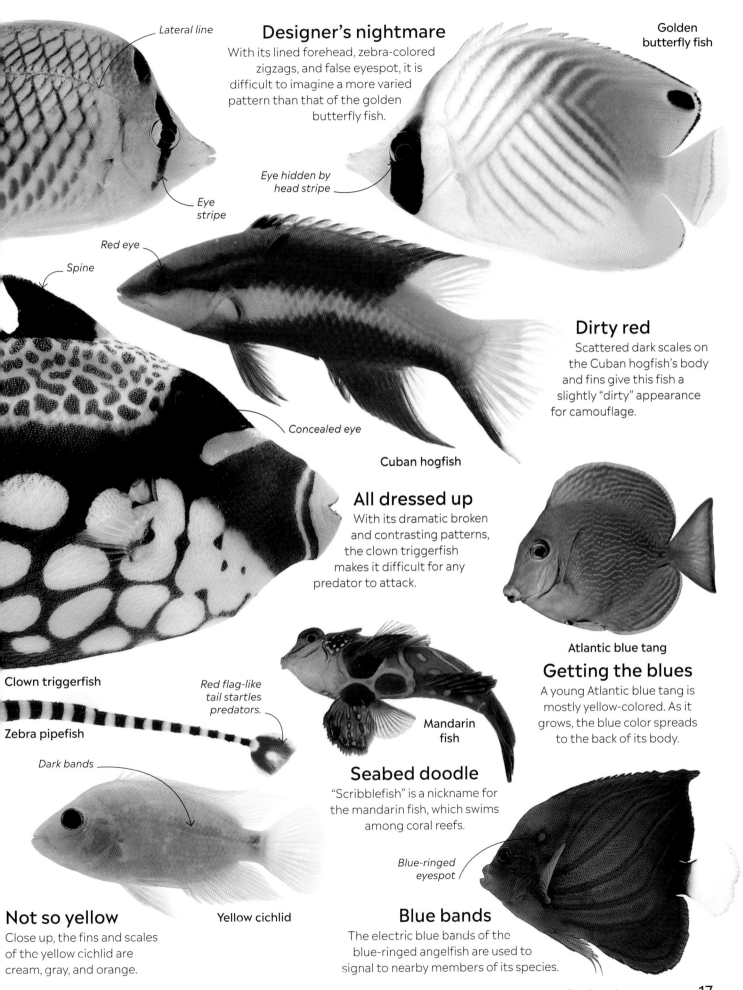

Lateral line

Designer's nightmare
With its lined forehead, zebra-colored zigzags, and false eyespot, it is difficult to imagine a more varied pattern than that of the golden butterfly fish.

Golden butterfly fish

Eye hidden by head stripe

Eye stripe

Red eye

Spine

Dirty red
Scattered dark scales on the Cuban hogfish's body and fins give this fish a slightly "dirty" appearance for camouflage.

Concealed eye

Cuban hogfish

All dressed up
With its dramatic broken and contrasting patterns, the clown triggerfish makes it difficult for any predator to attack.

Atlantic blue tang

Getting the blues
A young Atlantic blue tang is mostly yellow-colored. As it grows, the blue color spreads to the back of its body.

Clown triggerfish

Red flag-like tail startles predators.

Zebra pipefish

Dark bands

Mandarin fish

Seabed doodle
"Scribblefish" is a nickname for the mandarin fish, which swims among coral reefs.

Blue-ringed eyespot

Not so yellow
Close up, the fins and scales of the yellow cichlid are cream, gray, and orange.

Yellow cichlid

Blue bands
The electric blue bands of the blue-ringed angelfish are used to signal to nearby members of its species.

Continued on next page **17**

Continued from previous page

Cutting down on color

Surface-dwelling fish use countershading, which means they are dark on top and pale underneath. From above, they blend into the darker colors of deep water; from below, they merge into the shimmering surface water.

Rainbow trout

Crescent-shaped sheen

Rainbow colors

The rainbow trout is named after the crescent-shaped, pinkish band along the side of its body.

Golden scales

Golden brown

The crucian carp has large golden-brown scales, which blend in with murky weed-filled water.

Tench in a trench

Deep olive green, the bottom-living tench looks like a patch of murky water in weed-filled lakes.

Tench

Crucian carp

Thick tail base

Paler underside

Reddish fins

Silvery scales

Luminous organs

Most fish in dark ocean depths are jet black, and a lot of them, such as this loosejaw (left) and the Sloane's viperfish (below) have organs that light up. Flashing lights are used both to lure in prey and to confuse predators.

Rudd

Glimpsing a glint

In summer, the rudd swims near the surface catching insects. From above, its silvery sheen matches the glinting water.

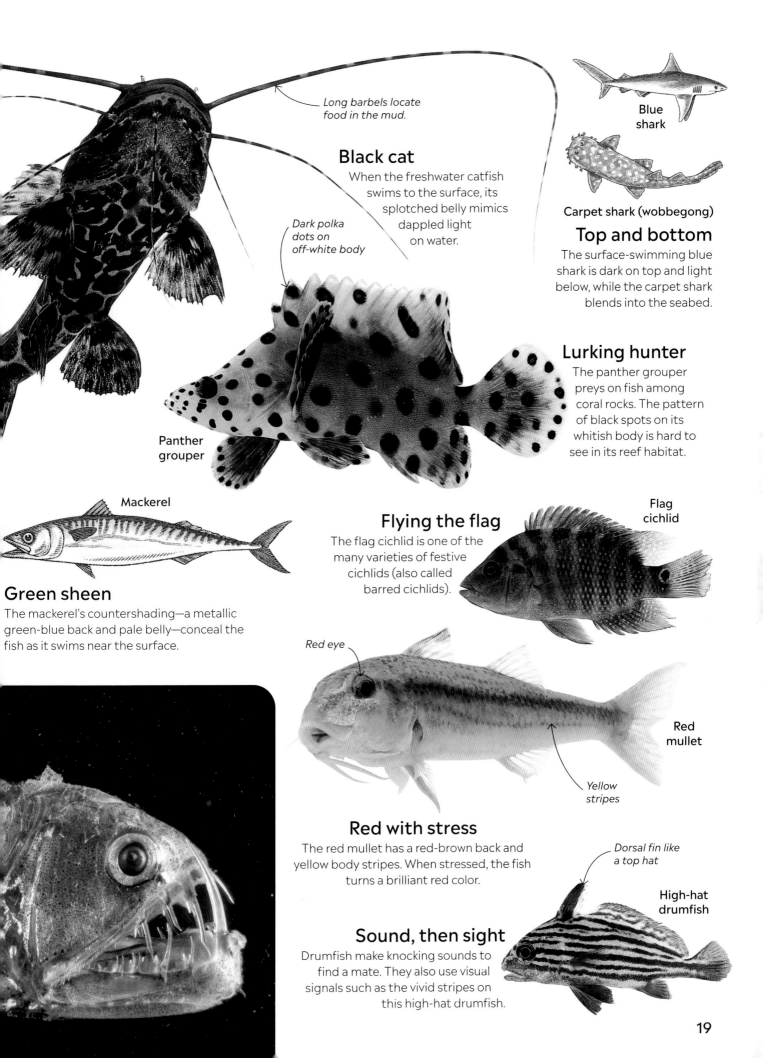

Long barbels locate food in the mud.

Black cat
When the freshwater catfish swims to the surface, its splotched belly mimics dappled light on water.

Dark polka dots on off-white body

Blue shark

Carpet shark (wobbegong)

Top and bottom
The surface-swimming blue shark is dark on top and light below, while the carpet shark blends into the seabed.

Lurking hunter
The panther grouper preys on fish among coral rocks. The pattern of black spots on its whitish body is hard to see in its reef habitat.

Panther grouper

Mackerel

Green sheen
The mackerel's countershading—a metallic green-blue back and pale belly—conceal the fish as it swims near the surface.

Flying the flag
The flag cichlid is one of the many varieties of festive cichlids (also called barred cichlids).

Flag cichlid

Red eye

Red mullet

Yellow stripes

Red with stress
The red mullet has a red-brown back and yellow body stripes. When stressed, the fish turns a brilliant red color.

Dorsal fin like a top hat

High-hat drumfish

Sound, then sight
Drumfish make knocking sounds to find a mate. They also use visual signals such as the vivid stripes on this high-hat drumfish.

19

Amazing shapes

Fish have evolved a variety of amazing shapes, from streamlined gars that dart through the water to squat frogfish that lurk on the seabed. Thin fish, such as the angelfish, slip between corals, while narrow shrimpfish swim among sea urchin spines. Shape can also be used for camouflage. Some fish look like plants, or even other animals.

Rocket fish
With its long snout and wide pectoral fins, the Harriott's longnose chimaera looks a little like a space rocket.

Long jaws

Straight as an arrow
With its streamlined shape, the longnose gar can move very fast to ambush prey—but only in short bursts.

Blade-shaped body
The clown knife fish has a long, deep body shaped like a carving knife. It swims using its long anal fin.

Thinly disguised
From the side, the European John Dory is disk-shaped, but head-on, its slim outline is hard to spot. This fish swims relatively slowly and tends to stalk its prey rather than chase it.

John Dory—front view

John Dory—side view

Gone fishing
The painted frogfish's wide, flat, knobbly body is ideal for lurking on the seabed.

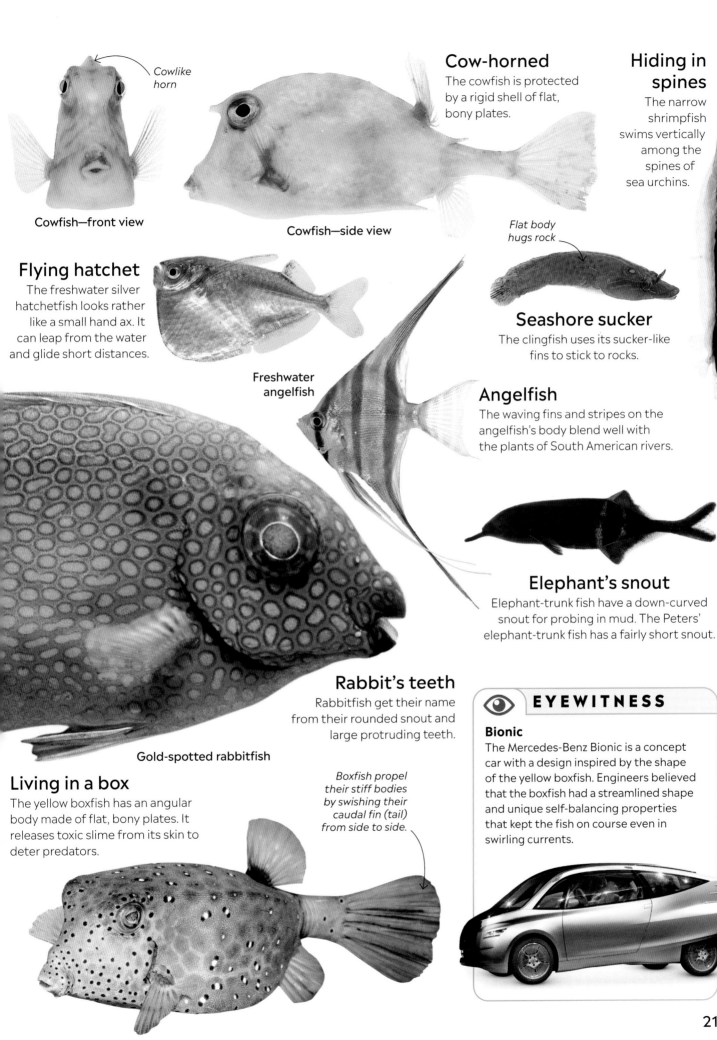

Cow-horned
The cowfish is protected by a rigid shell of flat, bony plates.

Cowlike horn

Cowfish—front view

Cowfish—side view

Hiding in spines
The narrow shrimpfish swims vertically among the spines of sea urchins.

Flying hatchet
The freshwater silver hatchetfish looks rather like a small hand ax. It can leap from the water and glide short distances.

Freshwater angelfish

Flat body hugs rock

Seashore sucker
The clingfish uses its sucker-like fins to stick to rocks.

Angelfish
The waving fins and stripes on the angelfish's body blend well with the plants of South American rivers.

Elephant's snout
Elephant-trunk fish have a down-curved snout for probing in mud. The Peters' elephant-trunk fish has a fairly short snout.

Rabbit's teeth
Rabbitfish get their name from their rounded snout and large protruding teeth.

Gold-spotted rabbitfish

Living in a box
The yellow boxfish has an angular body made of flat, bony plates. It releases toxic slime from its skin to deter predators.

Boxfish propel their stiff bodies by swishing their caudal fin (tail) from side to side.

Pipes and horses

With its horse-shaped head and ridged body, the seahorse swims upright, propelled through the water by its dorsal fin. Although it lacks pelvic and tail fins, it has a long, grasping tail that can grip seaweed. Its relative, the pipefish, is just as strange looking. Both creatures have an unusual method of reproduction. The female lays her eggs in a pouch or tube at the front of the male's body, where they develop into fully formed young.

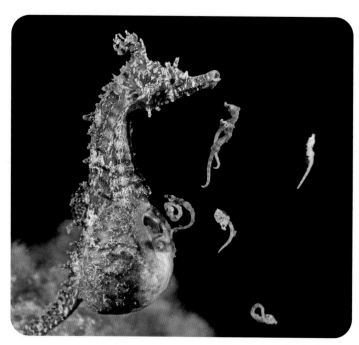

Pregnant father

As the breeding season approaches, the male's pouch becomes swollen. The female lays up to 2,000 eggs in the pouch. Two to six weeks later, the eggs develop into baby seahorses. First the opening of the pouch enlarges slightly and the male seahorse grasps a seagrass stem with his tail. He bends back and forth and baby seahorses shoot out in batches of five or so. Newborns of most species are ⅕–⅖ in (7–12 mm) long.

Hiding in the grass

Many seahorses can change color, from black or gray to bright yellow or orange. A seahorse hunts mainly by sight, sucking tiny water creatures into its tubular mouth. Its eyes can turn independently to view two scenes at once. Seahorses can remain still for long periods, secured by their prehensile tails and camouflaged among seaweeds or seagrasses as is the case with these lined seahorses.

Togetherness

Male and female pipefish court by swimming upright past each other. They then intertwine and she deposits the eggs in his pouch. Like most seahorses, some species of pipefish are monogamous and stay with the same partner throughout the breeding season.

Bony armor

Instead of scales, pipefish (right), seahorses, and sea dragons have bony plates for protection.

Resting in an upright position, the pipefish is well hidden.

Seahorse couples greet each other every day with a rhythmic dance routine.

Spot the pipefish

The pipefish's long, thin shape and green-brown color conceal it among the seaweeds. The male keeps the eggs in a tube formed by two flaps of skin along his abdomen. The babies are independent from the moment they hatch.

👁 EYEWITNESS

Heather Koldewey and Amanda Vincent
Cofounders of Project Seahorse, British marine biologist Heather Koldewey (left) and Canadian marine biologist Amanda Vincent (right) work with fishing communities and policymakers worldwide to conserve seahorses, pipefish, and sea dragons. These "umbrella species" help protect whole ecosystems.

Pipefish

Leaflike body parts

Long, tubelike snout

Tough, outer case

Weedy horse

Australasia's leafy sea dragon grows more than 12 in (30 cm) long. It is covered with fleshy flaps, making it hard to spot in shallow, weed-filled bays. The sea dragon is a weak swimmer and lacks the prehensile tail of seahorses.

Changing faces

Flatfish are not born flat. At first, they look much like any other larval fish. But within a few weeks, their bodies become thin and flat. The eye on one side gradually moves over to sit next to the eye on the opposite side. This leaves the underside of the fish "blind." The young fish sinks to the seabed, where it spends the rest of its life on its blind side.

A changing sole

The flatfish shown metamorphosing (changing) here is a European sole, which grows up to 24 in (60 cm) long.

1 Three days old

This side view of the baby sole shows the developing backbone. Actual size: ⅛ in (3.5 mm)

Yolk sac still visible

Eye

2 Five days old

The sole's left eye appears as a shadowy spot. The larval flatfish lives off nutrients in its yolk sac. Actual size: ⅛ in (3.5 mm)

Vertebrae begin to form.

3 Eight days old

The skull, jaw, and backbone develop further, and pigment cells grow in the skin. Actual size: ⅙ in (3.8 mm)

Pigment cells

11 Forty-five days

Nearly seven weeks after hatching, the young sole looks like its parent. Of the half million eggs released by the female, only one or two will become adults. Actual size: ⅖ in (11 mm)

Skin pigment cells form blotches of dark colour.

12 Nearly a year

The sole shows its changeable skin coloration under comb-edged scales.

10 Thirty-five days

The skull has grown more quickly on the left, causing that side to swing the left eye over to the right. Actual size: ⅜ in (10 mm)

Disappearing eyes

As young California blind gobies grow, their eyes disappear under the skin because they live in dark caves, where they do not need to use them.

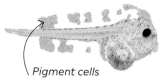

4 Ten days old

The larval sole now has a mouth that can open. Its fins run from the head almost to the tail. Actual size: ⅛ in (4 mm)

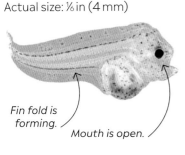

Fin fold is forming.

Mouth is open.

5 Thirteen days (right side)

The larva begins to feed on microscopic animals and plants. Actual size: ¼ in (5 mm)

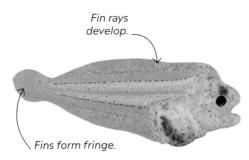

Fin rays develop.

Fins form fringe.

A deal of development

The newly hatched dealfish, only ½ in (15 mm) long, has very long fin rays. In the 8-ft (2.5-m) adult, the rays have completely disappeared.

6 Thirteen days (left side)

The left eye is moving toward the top of the head, and the skull and jaw are twisting around. The tail fin is more clearly defined. Actual size: ⅕ in (5 mm)

Left eye is migrating over head.

Tail fin

Left eye has moved to center of head.

7 Seventeen days (right side)

The left eye has moved to the center. The fish now eats the tiny larvae of other sea creatures. Actual size: ¼ in (6.5 mm)

Eye

Mouth

Mosaic patterning

Fringe of fins

Both eyes on right side of body

8 Twenty-two days

Both eyes are now on the right side of the body. The fish now has the sole's typically rounded head. Actual size: ⅜ in (8 mm)

Backbone

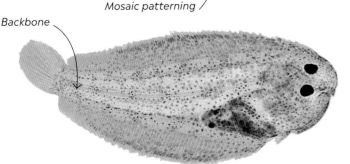

9 Twenty-eight days

What was once the right side is now the top side. The sole's skin is darkening. Actual size: ¾ in (9 mm)

Fish-handedness

Most members of a flatfish species have the same side facing upward. Turbots are "left-eyed," while most flounders are "right-eyed."

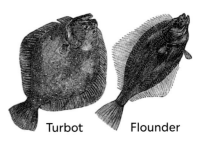

Turbot   **Flounder**

Continued on next page

Continued from previous page

Flatfish

Like most flatfish, the plaice lives on or near the seabed. It swims by flapping its entire body up and down in a wavelike motion. Then, it stiffens and glides down to the bottom, where it swishes its fins to brush up mud, sand, or gravel.

White side down

The plaice is a "right-eyed" flatfish—it keeps its blind left side flat against the seabed. As this side is not usually visible, it needs no pigment cells to color it.

Zigzag muscle blocks

Gill cover

Upper gill cover

Eyes on right side

Plaice face

Flatfish are not truly flat. The upper side is rounder, giving the fish a low, humped shape.

Front view of plaice

Small scales embedded in skin

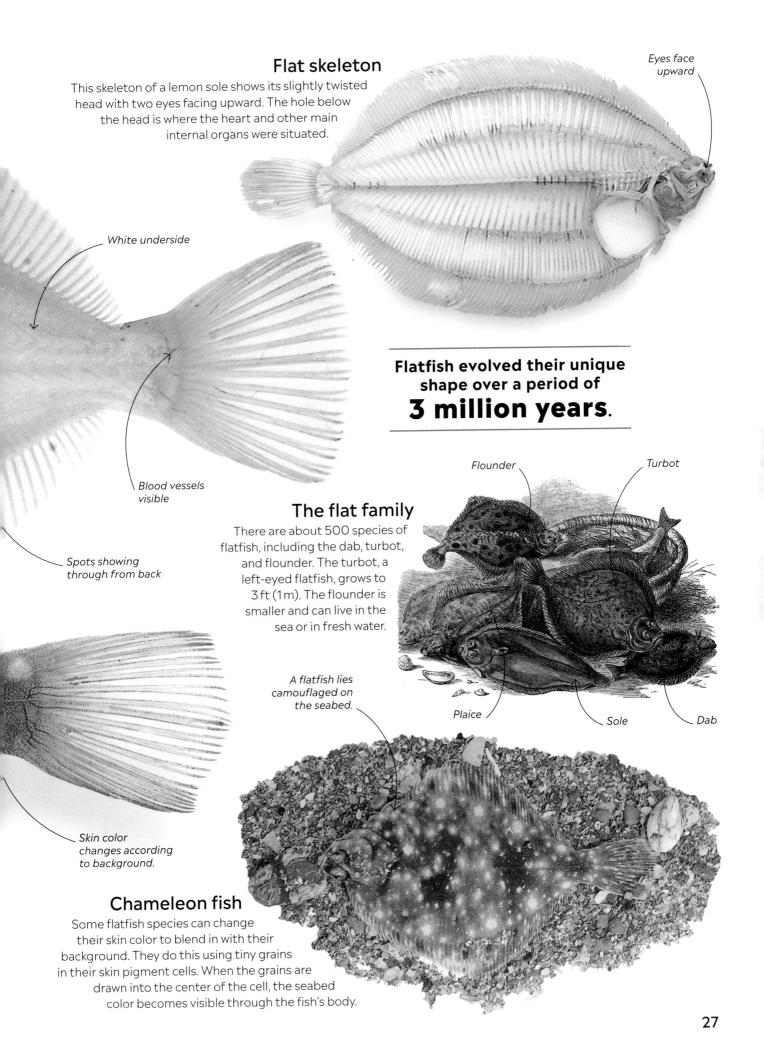

Flat skeleton

This skeleton of a lemon sole shows its slightly twisted head with two eyes facing upward. The hole below the head is where the heart and other main internal organs were situated.

Eyes face upward

White underside

Blood vessels visible

Spots showing through from back

Flatfish evolved their unique shape over a period of 3 million years.

The flat family

There are about 500 species of flatfish, including the dab, turbot, and flounder. The turbot, a left-eyed flatfish, grows to 3 ft (1 m). The flounder is smaller and can live in the sea or in fresh water.

Flounder

Turbot

Plaice

Sole

Dab

A flatfish lies camouflaged on the seabed.

Skin color changes according to background.

Chameleon fish

Some flatfish species can change their skin color to blend in with their background. They do this using tiny grains in their skin pigment cells. When the grains are drawn into the center of the cell, the seabed color becomes visible through the fish's body.

The art of swimming

A big splash
A great white shark can hurl its huge body out of the water, before falling back with a big splash. This is called "breaching."

Most fish swim by making a series of S-shaped "waves" that travel along the body. The wave begins with a small sideways motion of the head that becomes bigger as it sweeps toward the tail. The body and tail push the surrounding water sideways and backward, and so propel the fish forward. Most fish use their tails to move themselves forward, but some species "row" with their pectoral fins instead.

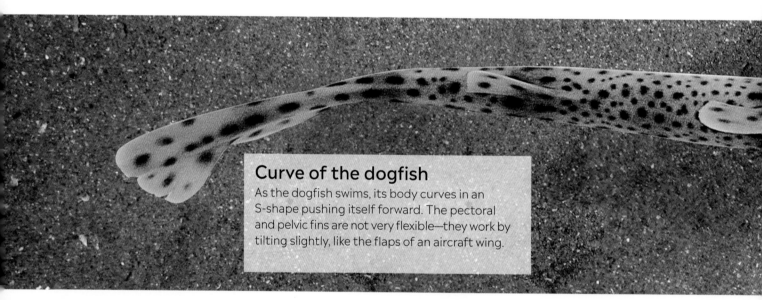

Curve of the dogfish
As the dogfish swims, its body curves in an S-shape pushing itself forward. The pectoral and pelvic fins are not very flexible—they work by tilting slightly, like the flaps of an aircraft wing.

"S" for swimming
This sequence of photographs, which cover about a second of time, shows the S-shaped wave passing along the body of a dogfish (a small shark).

The wave begins as the dogfish swings its head slightly to the right.

The "peak" of the wave has passed along the body to between the pectoral and pelvic fins.

Reversible eel
Eels swim in a similar way to the dogfish. However, an eel can reverse the direction of the S-shaped wave so that it travels from the tail to the head, allowing the eel to swim backward.

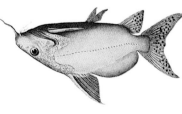

Reverse shading
The upside-down catfish has reverse countershading, with a dark belly and a pale back. The position of the lateral line when the fish is upside-down is shown in a related species (left).

Topsy-turvy fish

The mouth of the upside-down catfish is on the underside of its head, which is ideal for digging in the mud, but not for feeding from the surface. The fish solves this problem by turning over, so that it can catch flies from the water's surface.

The peak has now traveled to the pelvic and first dorsal fins.

As the peak reaches the area between the two dorsal fins, the tail begins its right thrust.

The wave's peak reaches the tail. Meanwhile the snout has begun another wave.

MOVING IN 3D

Fish use their fins to move forward and backward, left and right, and up and down. To change direction, the fish tilts its fins. The water presses on the fin to straighten it, producing a force that turns the fish's body.

Pitch
Pectoral and pelvic fins swivel to make the fish rise or dive.

Roll
Dorsal, pectoral, and pelvic fins make the fish roll.

Yaw
Different fin angles move the fish left or right.

Fin-driven ray

Most rays swim by waving the edges of their huge pectoral fins and "flying" through the water. Unlike fish, the S-shaped wave moves up and down rather than sideways.

Tails and **fins**

A fish uses its fins not only to swim forward and change direction, but also to stop and stand still. The shape of a fish's fins can provide clues to its way of life. A fish with slim side fins and a narrow forked tail, is probably a fast cruiser. A fish with broad side fins and a square-ended tail is probably a slow swimmer.

The tail is crescent-shaped for speed.

Sail tail
The sailfish is one of the fastest swimmers. Although its crescent-shaped tail is not very flexible, it is incredibly strong.

On tiptoe
The spiny rays of a tub gurnard's pectoral fins move like spider legs as the fish "tiptoes" on the seabed.

Stuck on sharks
The remora uses its dorsal fin as a sucker. It often sticks to a shark, feeding on its host's parasites.

Remora sucker

Long upper lobe

Unequal lobes
The sturgeon's uneven caudal fin is called a heterocercal tail—the fish's backbone extends upward into the upper lobe. Many sharks also have this kind of tail.

Unlikely tail
The tail of this butterfly fish from East Africa had marks that resembled old Arabic text saying "There is no God but Allah."

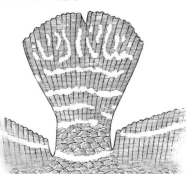

Fused tail
In some species of armored catfish, the upper and lower lobes of the tail fin are joined to form one large fin.

Butterfly fish tail

Sturgeon tail

Armored catfish tail

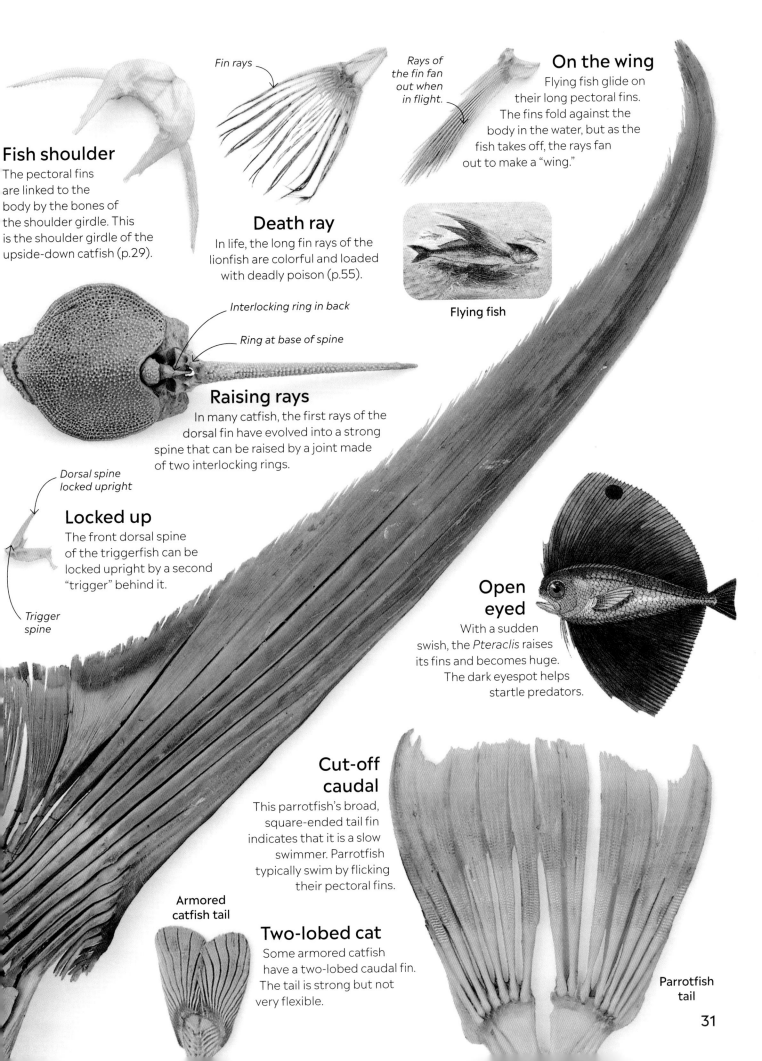

Fish shoulder

The pectoral fins are linked to the body by the bones of the shoulder girdle. This is the shoulder girdle of the upside-down catfish (p.29).

Fin rays

Death ray

In life, the long fin rays of the lionfish are colorful and loaded with deadly poison (p.55).

Rays of the fin fan out when in flight.

On the wing

Flying fish glide on their long pectoral fins. The fins fold against the body in the water, but as the fish takes off, the rays fan out to make a "wing."

Flying fish

Interlocking ring in back

Ring at base of spine

Raising rays

In many catfish, the first rays of the dorsal fin have evolved into a strong spine that can be raised by a joint made of two interlocking rings.

Dorsal spine locked upright

Locked up

The front dorsal spine of the triggerfish can be locked upright by a second "trigger" behind it.

Trigger spine

Open eyed

With a sudden swish, the *Pteraclis* raises its fins and becomes huge. The dark eyespot helps startle predators.

Cut-off caudal

This parrotfish's broad, square-ended tail fin indicates that it is a slow swimmer. Parrotfish typically swim by flicking their pectoral fins.

Armored catfish tail

Two-lobed cat

Some armored catfish have a two-lobed caudal fin. The tail is strong but not very flexible.

Parrotfish tail

Fish with legs

Although most fish move by swimming, some can "walk," using their fins as legs. Others can leave the water for periods of time and breathe on land. Mudskippers, for example, "skip" across coastal mudflats and mangrove swamps. Some African catfish elbow their way across land, like soldiers crawling on their chests. Some fish, such as climbing perches, can absorb oxygen directly from the air. They gulp air into the mouth and throat where the oxygen is absorbed by a rich supply of blood vessels.

Fins like oars

Blennies use their strong pectoral fins as oars to "row" across rock if they become stranded out of water.

Moist muddy surface

Male mudskippers
leap in the air
to attract mates.

Mangrove trunks

Legless fish

Edward Lear's strange "fizzigiggious fish" character walked on stilts because he had no legs!

A thick layer of clear skin protects bulging eyes.

Fish with lungs

Equipped with lungs as well as gills, lungfish can breathe out of water. This African lungfish has burrowed into mud and made a cocoon of mucus to keep in moisture. During the drought, the fish breathes through a porous mud plug at the top of the burrow.

African lungfish hibernating

Unlike other lungfish, the Australian lungfish cannot hibernate to survive drought.

Fish on stilts

The deep-sea tripod fish's pelvic fins and lower tail fin extend into long, stiff filaments. It props itself up on these, like stilts, to stand on the seabed.

Fin rays

To keep eyes moist when out of the water, mudskippers can roll them back into the moist sockets.

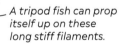

A tripod fish can prop itself up on these long stiff filaments.

EYEWITNESS

Richard Blob, Ben McInroe, and Dan Goldman
Scientists Richard Blob (left), Ben McInroe (center), and Dan Goldman (right) teamed up to build Muddybot, a robotic mudskipper, which showed that a mudskipper's tail plays a key role in its ability to "walk" out of the water. This could help better understand how early vertebrates first moved from seas to land.

A walk in the mud

In this coastal swamp in Southeast Asia, small pop-eyed creatures scurry across the surface, catching insects. These mudskippers can prop themselves up and skip quickly on their muscular pectoral fins. They can stay on land for hours, holding water in their gills and absorbing oxygen through their mouth and throat.

Short, muscular pectoral fins look like stubby legs out of water.

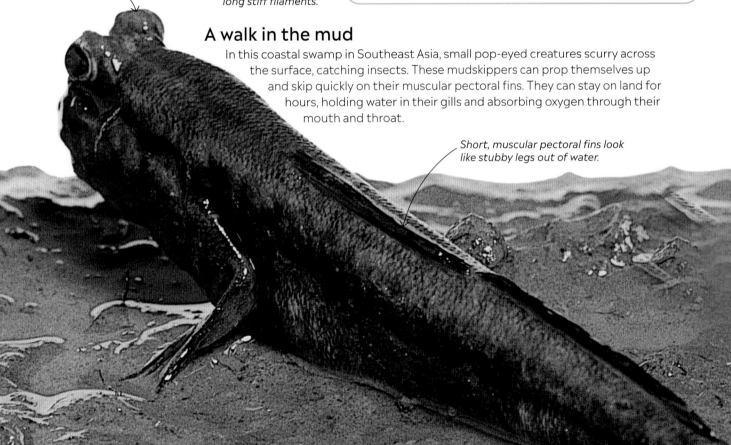

Sharp nose

A swordfish's snout is typically more than 13 ft (4 m) long. Young swordfish have a relatively short snout that gradually develops into the flattened "sword." The sword is used to stun rather than impale prey.

Fish feeding

The food chain in water begins with tiny, floating algae called phytoplankton. This plankton provides food for microscopic animals, who are eaten in turn by small creatures such as shrimp. The head and teeth of a fish can provide clues to its diet. Flat, crushing teeth indicate a diet of shellfish or corals, while sharp, pointed teeth indicate a hunting lifestyle.

The bloodsucker

The jawless lamprey scrapes its prey's flesh with its teeth and sucks the blood.

Rows of sharp teeth help grip the prey.

Porcupine fish skull

Fused teeth

The porcupine fish feeds on hard-shelled mussels, shellfish, and even spiny sea urchins. In each jaw, the teeth are fused to form a hard biting ridge at the front, with a flat crushing plate behind.

Hard-shelled mussel

A fanciful engraving of a swordfish with a victim impaled on its "sword"

Swordfish nose (rostral bone)

Poking its nose in

The elephant-trunk fish has a long, curved "nose" with tiny jaws at the end. It pokes its snout into mud to find prey.

Elephant-trunk fish skull

Tiny jaws

Sharp saw

The sawfish's razor-sharp teeth sit in cartilage sockets. It uses its "saw" for probing into the seabed for food.

Sharp teeth in cartilage sockets

Sawfish snout

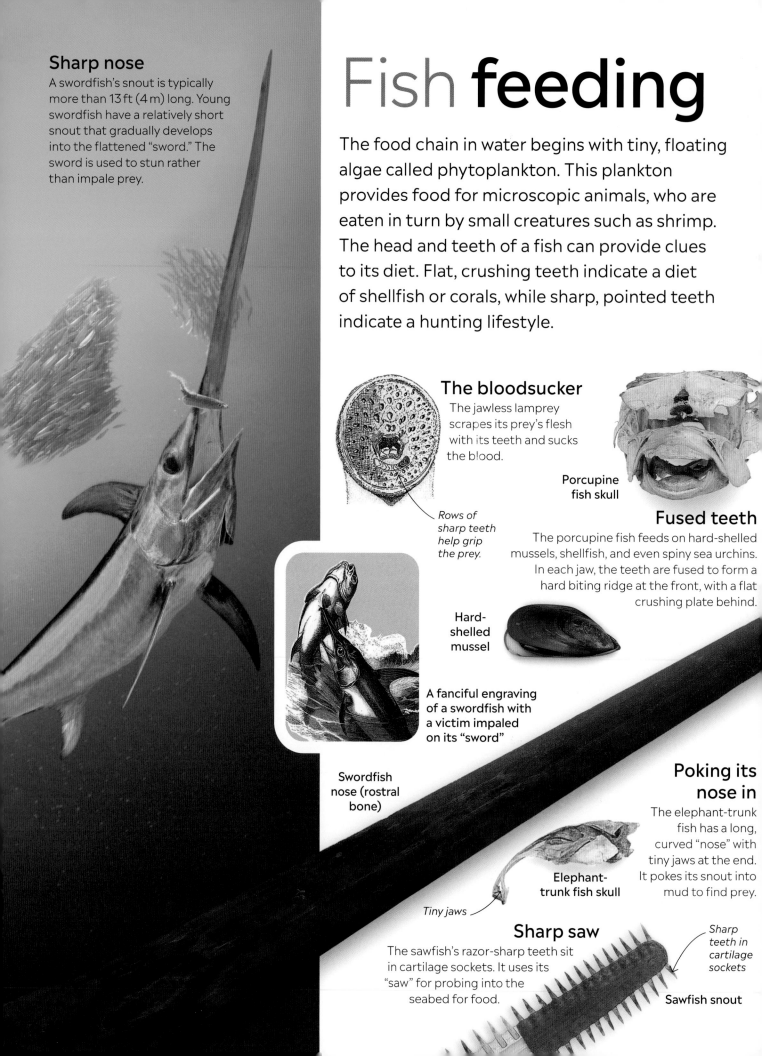

Chewing throat

The European bream has a "pouting" mouth to suck up worms and insect larvae. These are then ground up by teeth in its throat.

European bream skull

Pouting mouth for sucking in food

Throat teeth of bream

Fruit and nuts

The Brazilian pacu has strong, crushing teeth. It feeds on fruit and nuts that fall into the water.

Strong, crushing teeth

Seed of *Piranhea trifoliata* (the piranha tree)

Brazil nuts

Sharp, daggerlike teeth

Small, razor-sharp teeth shred prey, while large teeth are used to grip and pierce.

John Dory skull

Beware the barracuda

Barracudas are fearsome predators that swim in warmer oceans. They use their sharp, spear-like teeth to seize and tear up other fish. Larger barracudas, which grow to nearly 10 ft (3 m) long, have been known to attack humans. However, they rarely strike unless provoked.

Surprising jaws

The European John Dory swims head-on toward smaller fish and shrimp. Then its great jaws suddenly lunge forward to engulf the prey.

Shrimp

Teeth lock together for a clean bite.

Wide mouth on top of head

Fangs

The South American piranha can devour prey in minutes with its triangular, bladelike teeth.

Coral crushers

Reef fish feed in a variety of ways. The parrotfish uses its horny "beak" to scrape algae off rocks. The tapered snout of the forceps fish is ideal for poking in crevices. Both the triggerfish and the leatherjacket have chisel-like teeth to bore holes in shells.

Stony faced

The stonefish lies hidden on the seabed, gulping unwary prey into its wide mouth.

Trumpet fish skull with long snout

Trumpet fish tweezers

The trumpet fish uses its long snout and tiny teeth like tweezers to pull small creatures out of their hiding places.

Horny beak

Parrotfish skull

Coral

Forceps fish skull

Leatherjacket skull

Triggerfish skull

Food out of water

Most fish feed in water. Some, such as trout, rise to the surface to snatch insects. But a few can catch prey on land, or even in trees. Archerfish, found in mangrove swamps from India to Australasia, can squirt a jet of water droplets at insects and other creatures sitting on leaves above the surface. The surprise attack knocks the prey into the water, where the archerfish snaps it up.

Spider on leaf is the prey.

Jet of water aimed at the spider

WATER-JET PUMP

The archerfish presses its tongue against a groove in the roof of its mouth. Then it snaps its gill covers shut, forcing a jet of water out of its mouth.

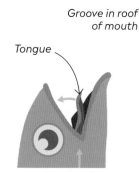

Tongue

Groove in roof of mouth

Side view of archerfish's mouth

Roof of archerfish's mouth

A direct hit

The archerfish tilts its body vertically and shoots out a jet of water. If the first jet misses, the fish adjusts its aim and shoots again. Archerfish begin to "spit" when very young, although their jets only travel about 4 in (10 cm).

An adult archerfish can accurately shoot water from its mouth to hit its prey up to a distance of 5 ft (1.5 m).

The spider on the leaf is about to be snapped up by an archerfish.

Archerfish have large eyes and excellent eyesight.

Freshwater butterfly fish

The fish's long, raylike pelvic fins often hang straight down as it floats just below the water's surface.

Leaping for its supper

Archerfish not only shoot at prey, they can also leap out of the water and knock flying insects down. In an aquarium, they have been known to jump at food stuck to the glass 12 in (30 cm) above the water's surface. They may sometimes even jump or squirt at people leaning over to watch them!

Leaping butterfly

The West African butterfly fish can leap out of the water to catch a tasty morsel at heights of more than 6 ft (2 m)—some feat for a fish no longer than 4 in (10 cm)!

Aerial hunter

Deep in the Amazon's waters lurks the arowana, an agile fish with a large, scoop-like mouth. Like the archerfish, the arowana can leap clear of the water to catch a small bird or bat flying just above.

Rising to the occasion

Trout often rise to the surface to feed on drowning flies or other food trapped at the surface.

Scaring the enemy

Fish are always on the alert for predators. Speed is one way to foil the hunter. Size is another—very big fish are often too much of a mouthful, and tiny ones can hide in cracks and crevices. Some fish have evolved clever weapons to defend themselves. Porcupine fish can inflate their bodies and raise their spines, while triggerfish have a rigid spine on the back with which they wedge themselves inside crevices in the coral reef, making it hard for a predator to pull them out.

Light for life

Many deep-sea fish have luminous organs that can protect them from predators. This scaled dragonfish has light-producing organs lining the side of its body, and their light can confuse larger predators.

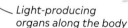

Light-producing organs along the body

The surgeon's scalpel

Surgeonfish get their name from the two sharp structures, called lancets, in front of the tail. If threatened, the fish suddenly flicks out its tail, slicing the lancets into the enemy's flesh. In some species, the blades lie folded in a groove when not in use.

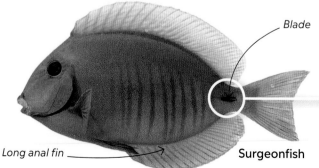

Blade

Long anal fin

Surgeonfish

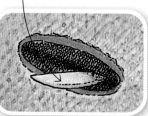

The blade extends at right angles to the fish.

The spines lie flat when the fish is at rest.

Going up

A "relaxed" porcupine fish (above) looks much like many other fish. But when threatened, it can raise its spines to make itself a prickly mouthful (left). It can also quickly take in water and balloon to two or three times its normal size—making it too large for most predators to swallow. Its relative, the puffer fish (below), also inflates its body, but has shorter spines than the porcupine fish.

Normal shape of puffer fish

The length of the fish remains unchanged after puffing up.

Puffer fish inflated to full extent

The spines swivel out when the porcupine fish is inflated.

The pale underside color is more pronounced when inflated.

A porcupine fish's spines are
modified
bony scales.

Setting up house

Like other baby animals, baby fish develop from the eggs of the female, which are fertilized by the male. Some species carry out dramatic courtship routines to attract a mate, such as changing color or performing elaborate dances. Most fish leave their eggs to hatch on their own, but some, such as the three-spined stickleback, build nests to give the eggs and young a better chance of survival.

At the seaside
A male black goby guards his nest on the seabed until the eggs hatch.

Red and blue breeders

In the breeding season, the male three-spined stickleback develops a deep-red throat and bright-blue eyes. He builds a nest for the female's eggs, which he fertilizes and guards until the young hatch and can fend for themselves.

Piece of water plant

Bright-blue eye

Red throat

1 Nest materials
The male stickleback collects pieces of water plants.

Nest at sea

The male sea stickleback makes a nest, like its freshwater cousin. The fish puts bits of seaweed in a large clump and then "ropes" it together with sticky thread made by its kidneys.

The sand circle is 6½ ft (2 m) across and takes the male puffer a week to make.

Warning displays

The male stops occasionally to perform quick motions such as these (left) to warn other fish to stay away.

"Yawn" display

"S-bend" display

The stickleback shovels gravel with his snout.

2 Digging the foundation
He pushes his snout into the stones to make a shallow hole. The nests are often built beneath small boulders.

A boulder shelters the nest.

3 A firm base
He prods the plant pieces firmly with his snout to make a secure base.

The stickleback prods weeds into place with his snout.

Complicated courting

A male white-spotted puffer fish bites a female while she lays eggs in his seabed nest. The furrows in the sand channel oxygen-rich water into the center of the nest where the eggs develop. The male guards them for up to six days until they hatch.

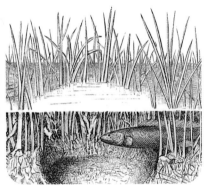

Paternal instinct

The male bowfin makes a nest of gravel and bits of plant. The hatched larvae attach themselves to the nest by glue glands on their heads, until they are ready to swim free.

Blowing bubbles

The dwarf gourami is a bubble-nest breeder. After fertilizing his partner's eggs, the male blows them into a mass of floating saliva-coated bubbles, where they begin to develop.

4 Cement stage

As the nest material grows, the male cements it together with a sticky substance made by his kidneys.

5 Added ventilation

The fish fans a current of fresh water through the nest to bring oxygen to the eggs.

Fanlike pectoral fins create a current of water.

Fish eggs

Most bony fish release millions of eggs into the water, which are left to fend for themselves. In contrast, the bullhead lays only one or two hundred eggs, which the male guards fiercely as they hatch into fry (young). Not all fish lay eggs. Some species, including some sharks, are viviparous, like mammals. This means that the embryos (babies) grow inside the mother's body and she gives birth to fully formed young.

Female ocean sunfish can release
300 million eggs
at a time, more than any other fish.

Broad, flat head

Wide pectoral fins are ideal for fanning and aerating the eggs.

Cannibal bullhead

In the spring, clumps of round, yellowish eggs appear in stony holes in rivers and lakes across Europe. These are the egg masses of the female bullhead. The male guards the eggs for up to a month as they hatch and the young begin to swim. However, any babies leaving later than one month are eaten by their father!

Round, yellowish clump of eggs

Inside the egg

These magnified eggs are of the three-spined stickleback (p.40), seven days after fertilization. In life they are about 1/16 in (2 mm) across. The developing embryo lives on the yolk sac until its organs have formed.

Tendrils help attach the egg case to seaweed or rocks.

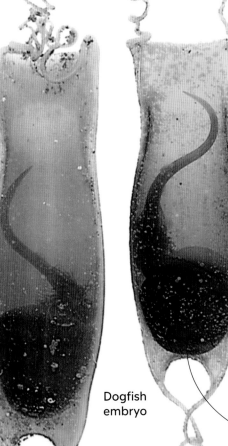

Dogfish embryo

Male bullhead guarding clumps of eggs on rock

Dogfish and her egg cases

Born from a purse

The hard, horny "mermaid's purses" found on beaches are usually the empty egg cases of dogfish, skates, and rays. The female lays her eggs in the cases, which are attached to seaweeds by long, curling tendrils.

The yolk provides nutrients to the developing embryo.

CASE COLLECTION

Egg cases vary according to the type of fish that lays them. The chimaera (p.20) produces a long tadpole-like case; the bottom-dwelling Port Jackson shark from Australia has a distinctive corkscrew-shaped case; while the spotted ray's case is more like the common "mermaid's purse"

Chimaera egg case

Port Jackson shark egg case

Spotted ray egg case

Black caviar from beluga sturgeon

Red caviar from salmon

Eggs on toast

Some fish eggs have become delicacies in the form of caviar. However, the fishing of females for caviar is threatening species such as the beluga sturgeon.

Attentive parents

Some species of fish take great care to protect their young. Fish known as mouthbreeders carry the eggs in their mouth and throat, while seahorse and pipefish fathers hold the eggs in a pouch. Sharks also protect their pups. Some shark pups are born in special nursery grounds, such as the mangroves of the Bahamas, which are nurseries for lemon shark pups. Adult male sharks rarely come to the area, and the females do not feed at this time, ensuring a safe start for most pups.

Brood pouch
The Asian bonytongue, *Scleropages*, looks after its eggs and young in a large pouch-like part of its lower jaw. Newly hatched larvae live in the male's mouth for 7–8 weeks.

Making a nest
The male blue Malawi dolphin cichlid clears a shallow hole in the lake bed for the female to lay her eggs. The female carries the eggs in her mouth until they hatch.

Young cichlid being "blown" out of mother's mouth

Mouthbreeders
This term describes a group of fish that carry their eggs in their mouth. Even after hatching, the young remain in the safety of their mother's "mouth nursery." The banded yellow mouthbreeder (right) is a cichlid, and lives in Africa's Lake Malawi.

Out of mother's mouth
This banded yellow mouthbreeder "blows" her babies from her mouth, giving both mother and young a chance to feed. As they grow, the fry venture out more, until they only return to her mouth at night or when in danger.

Stirring up mud

The male African lungfish makes a deep pit for the female's eggs in swampy mud. He fiercely protects the hatchlings for up to two months by snapping at and chasing predators. He also swishes fresh water through the nest by writhing his body.

Clinging on

Many young creatures, including mammals such as monkeys, cling to their parents. The fry of the blue discus fish (below) are no different.

Close to
2,000 species of cichlids
have been identified, most of them in the Great Lakes of Africa.

The fry feed on mucus secreted by both male and female parents.

Parent nibblers

A week after hatching, the fry of the blue discus fish start to feed on special secretions made by their parents' skin. Parent-nibbling continues for about four weeks until the young swim away.

Bright yellow bands of color give this mouthbreeder its name.

Cichlids remain near their mother in case danger threatens.

Living in
harmony

Many fish develop special relationships with others in return for benefits such as food, grooming, or protection. Tiny fish called cleaners scrape off parasites, dead skin, and scales from the jaws of much bigger fish in exchange for a meal. Similarly, clown fish and damselfish take refuge among poisonous sea anemone tentacles, while the anemone absorbs pieces of food dropped by its guests.

Tiny companions
Little pilot fish swim alongside sharks and eat their parasites. The pilot fish are then protected from predators who won't swim near the sharks.

Clown fish never stray far from the protection of the anemones.

Two black-ray goby fish emerge from a burrow built by a Randall's pistol shrimp (bottom).

Partners
The goby fish and the pistol shrimp have a relationship that benefits both of them. The shrimp digs a burrow for itself and the goby fish, and keeps it clean. In turn, the goby fish stands guard and watches for predators, flicking its tail fin on the shrimp's antennae as a warning if danger approaches.

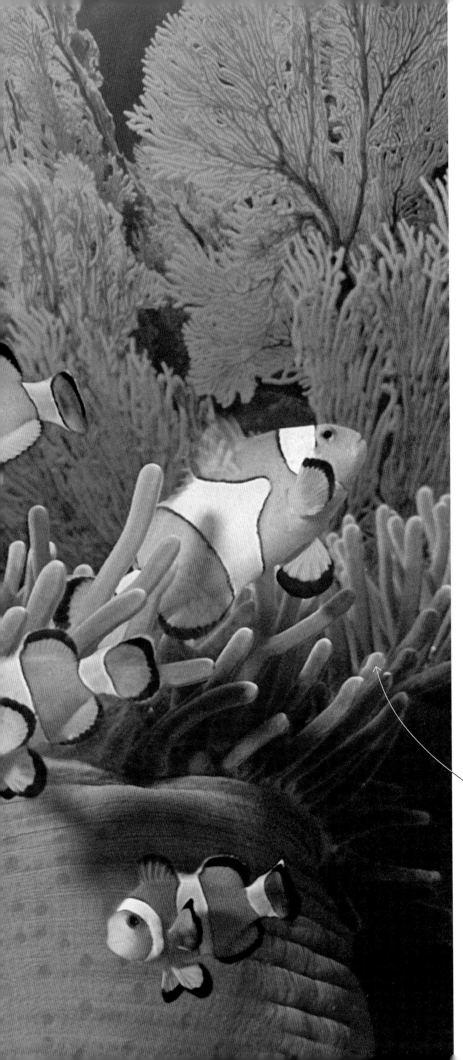

Cleaner at work

Cleaner fish, such as some wrasses, pick pieces of dead skin and scales, and parasites, from the skin, gills, and mouths of larger fish. Here, a tiny bluestreak cleaner wrasse attends to a tomato grouper in the Indian Ocean near the coast of Indonesia.

Clown fish help anemones by stirring up oxygen-rich water and chasing away predators, such as the butterfly fish, that feed on anemone tentacles.

Anemones use their stinging cells to catch and eat fish that may prey on the brightly colored clown fish.

Clowning around

Sea anemone tentacles bear venomous stings that can paralyze other small fish in seconds. Clown fish survive in this environment probably because they have a thick covering of mucus that prevents them from being stung. However, clown fish are not immune to all types of anemone. A sting from the fire anemone is particularly deadly.

Snakes of the sea

Skin is slimy and slippery.

Pelican eel

The deep-water pelican eel has a huge mouth and a tiny body.

Slimy, wormlike eels resemble snakes more than fish. There are about 600 species of true eels, including freshwater eels, congers, morays, and gulpers. Other fish groups have their own eel-shaped members, such as the South American electric eel. Perhaps the most intriguing thing about eels is their breeding pattern, which remained a mystery until Danish zoologist Johannes Schmidt tracked the migration route of European eels in the 1920s.

Front nostril

Yellow dorsal fin of ribbon eel

A tight fit

The brightly colored ribbon eel is a type of moray. It seizes prey with a fast, snakelike strike. The eel can coil itself backward into crevices that seem far too small for its long body.

The serpent's tale

For centuries, sailors have told of terrifying "sea serpents." Some of these sightings may have been of oarfish, which can grow more than 20 ft (6 m) long.

Electric eels are practically blind and use weak electric signals as a radar to move around.

Stunning eel

The body of the electric eel has up to 6,000 electroplates—modified muscles arranged like tiny batteries. The eel can kill small fish with 500-volt shocks.

Thick, scaleless body

Moray's foray

Moray eels grow to 10 ft (3 m) long and are often brightly colored.

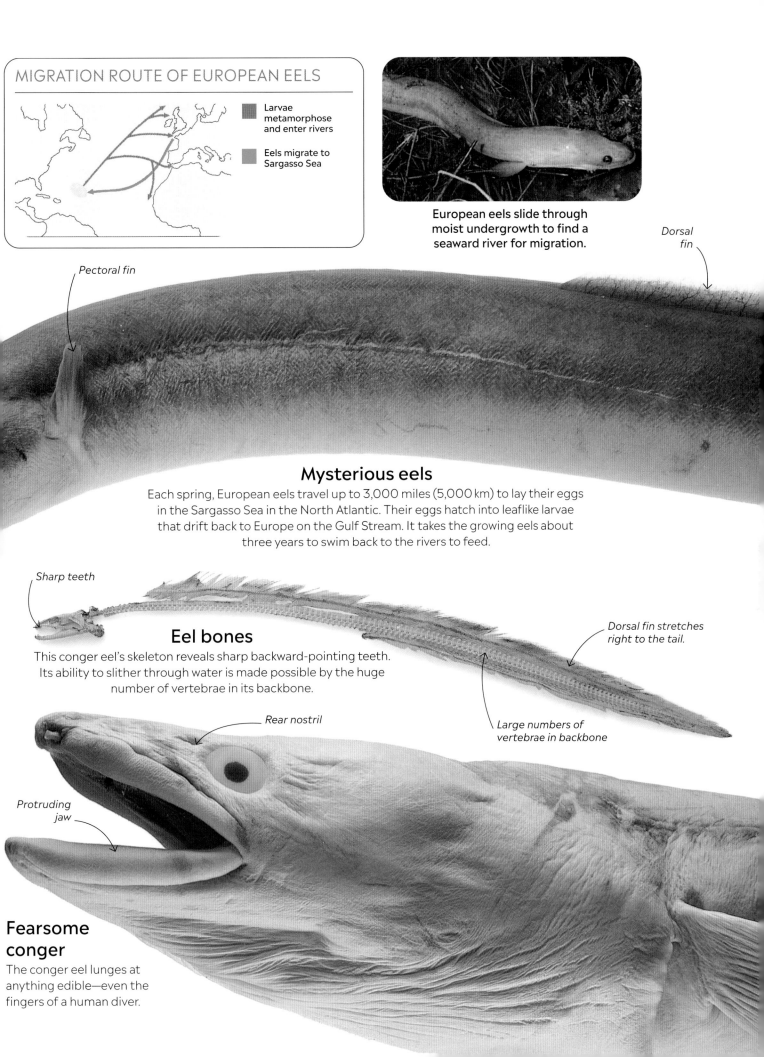

MIGRATION ROUTE OF EUROPEAN EELS

■ Larvae metamorphose and enter rivers

■ Eels migrate to Sargasso Sea

European eels slide through moist undergrowth to find a seaward river for migration.

Dorsal fin

Pectoral fin

Mysterious eels

Each spring, European eels travel up to 3,000 miles (5,000 km) to lay their eggs in the Sargasso Sea in the North Atlantic. Their eggs hatch into leaflike larvae that drift back to Europe on the Gulf Stream. It takes the growing eels about three years to swim back to the rivers to feed.

Sharp teeth

Dorsal fin stretches right to the tail.

Eel bones

This conger eel's skeleton reveals sharp backward-pointing teeth. Its ability to slither through water is made possible by the huge number of vertebrae in its backbone.

Large numbers of vertebrae in backbone

Rear nostril

Protruding jaw

Fearsome conger

The conger eel lunges at anything edible—even the fingers of a human diver.

Hiding places

The "landscape" of the underwater world is made up of seaweed gardens, dazzling reefs, and rocky cliffs. Each of these habitats offers hiding places for both predators and prey. Most of the hunted feed out in the open, but within seconds they can dig into burrows or dive between rocks. Many hunters are content to lurk in cracks or caves, watching for unwary victims to swim by.

Locked file

The first spine of the filefish's dorsal fin has tiny notches. When in trouble, the fish swims into a crevice and locks its dorsal spine upright. It is then wedged in and almost impossible to remove.

Safe in the sand

The twinspot wrasse, from tropical reefs, has two large eyespots on its dorsal fin. If this huge "face" does not frighten the predator, the twinspot can dive into the coral sand or gravel and be out of sight within a few seconds.

White and orange colors change to dark green as the fish grows older.

The wrasse's body is in a horizontal position and already throwing up gravel.

Eyespots give the illusion of a big "face".

The wrasse searches for a loose patch of gravel.

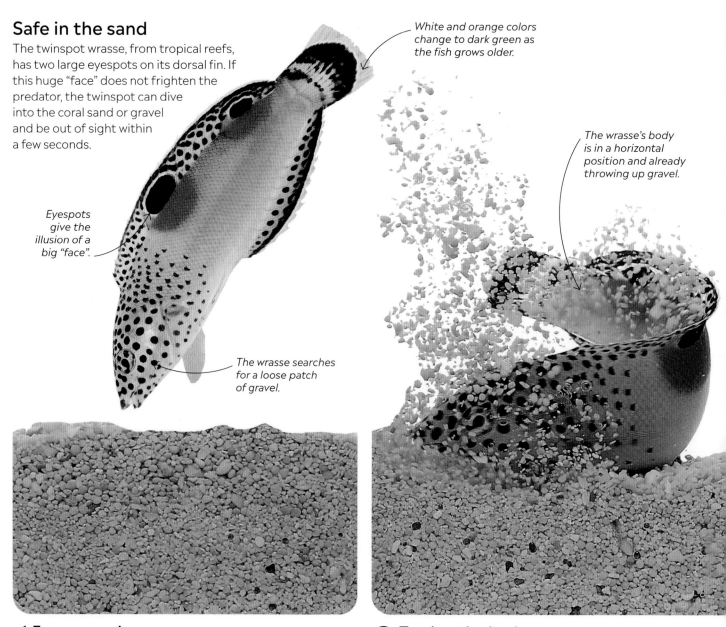

1 Emergency!
The twinspot detects danger. At once it tilts its head down and searches out a patch of gravel for refuge.

2 Testing the bed
As the fish reaches the seabed it becomes horizontal and thrusts its sensitive snout and chest into the gravel. If this turns out to be only a shallow layer on top of solid rock the twinspot needs to find a new spot without delay!

Human-made litter is treated with suspicion until it is slowly hidden in weeds and other creatures.

Vanishing garden

As they sway in the current, garden eels look more like plants than a group of fish. With its rear end rooted in its burrow, the eel snaps at drifting plants and animals. When disturbed, the eels sink swiftly into their burrows and the entire "garden" disappears.

Bottled up

This goby has taken refuge in the neck of a bottle. As the bottle gets encrusted with weeds, it becomes a "cave" for fish hiding from predators, or for hunters waiting to ambush prey.

One-third of this whitespotted garden eel's body is always buried in the sand.

Loose gravel flung upward by wrasse's activity

A single garden eel colony can have
hundreds or thousands
of individuals.

The body is in an S-shaped curve, to burrow more efficiently.

Part of the wrasse's body is still visible in this photograph (but invisible to predators).

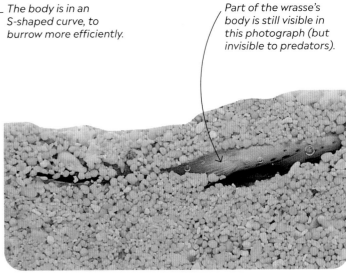

3 Digging in

Digging in a diagonal direction, the wrasse "swims" head first into the loose gravel. It flings the gravel upward out of the way.

4 Out of sight, out of mind

Within a few seconds, the fish is settled into the pebbles until the danger is over. Many species of wrasse bury themselves in gravel each night to rest. Others lie on their sides in caves and crevices.

Life on the move

Many fish swim together in loose groups called shoals or schools where fish move in unison. Grouping helps fish find food and navigate when migrating. Schools often swim together for protection. Predators can become confused by the huge numbers of fish and find it difficult to pick out individual prey. Many schools move as one with the help of visual markers, such as spots or stripes on the body. The lateral line also provides information about neighbors' movements.

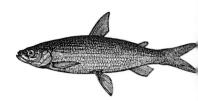

Swimming schools
Hundreds of thousands of Atlantic herring meet up to spawn each year off the northeast coast of the US. They move in a precise arrangement to maintain a cruising speed.

Food chain
Groups of Pacific herring swim in schools to avoid predators such as California sea lions. Herring are a vital link in ocean food chains, as they are prey for many fish and seabirds. In the days of sailboat fishing (left), herring catches were fairly constant. But since the arrival of school-locating radar, herring numbers have declined due to overfishing.

Darker back for countershading (p.18)

Silvery side

White underside

Dashing habits of this fish give it the nickname of dart.

Eyes can look up and down.

School as a whole

Common dace live in fast, clear, rivers across Europe. They often swim in large schools, especially when young. The fish dart and turn in formation, moving together as a single unit. In summer they swim just below the surface, coming up to catch flies and other insects.

Dwindling tuna

The great tuna schools have dwindled in numbers today, mainly due to overfishing.

Bait ball hunting

A striped marlin (right) hunts sardines in a tight swarm called a bait ball. Each sardine tries to avoid the marlin by swimming toward the center of the ball.

A shoal can have a mix of fish, but fish in a school are all the same species.

Poisonous fish

Up to 3,000 kinds of venomous fish swim in the world's waters. Every year, people become severely ill, or even die, from the poison of stingrays, weevers, lionfish, and other species. But these fish did not evolve their venom in order to harm humans. They use it mainly as a defense against larger predators such as big flatfish and rays.

Sting in the tail

More than 100 species of stingray lurk in coastal shallows. Some grow very large, with a "wingspan" of more than 10 ft (3 m). When in danger, these rays attack with their stinger—a hard "dagger" of bone set into the tail. The ray swings its tail or arches it over its head, slashing its stinger into the enemy. Its poison acts quickly on humans, causing pain, numbness, or even death.

Eye

The ray's sting

The stinger's venom comes from the shiny, white tissue running along grooves under the spine.

Barbed stinger on tail

Large pectoral fin

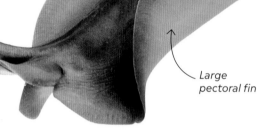

Be wary of the weever

The lesser weever lies half buried in the sand, waiting for food. If attacked, or trodden on, venom flows from glands at the base of spines on the gill covers and first dorsal fin.

Dinner or death?

Certain types of puffer fish are poisonous to humans when eaten. In Japan, specially trained chefs serve puffer fish as the delicacy fugu. Despite safeguards, some people become severely ill and even die from eating incorrectly prepared fugu.

Japanese diners eating fugu

A sharp eye is needed to identify the poisonous organs.

Deadly beauty

The graceful, brightly colored lionfish is one of the most venomous creatures in the sea. Glands in the spiny rays of its lacy fins make a venom that can paralyze a predator but rarely kills a human. It can grow up to 16 in (40 cm) long and inhabits warm, shallow waters. Lionfish are native to the Indian and Pacific Oceans, but people have introduced them to the Caribbean and the Mediterranean, where they are disrupting many ecosystems.

Thirteen venomous dorsal spines

Three venomous anal spines

Stony faced

The stonefish has a warty, blotched body that blends perfectly with the stony seabed. When threatened, the fish raises spines along its back. Stonefish spines can inject the most potent of all fish venoms.

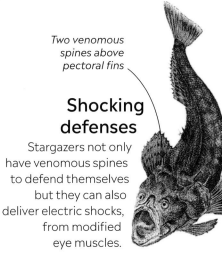

Two venomous spines above pectoral fins

Shocking defenses

Stargazers not only have venomous spines to defend themselves but they can also deliver electric shocks, from modified eye muscles.

SHEATHED SPINE

A sheath on the lionfish spine is pushed down when it enters the victim. This disrupts the glandular tissue and releases venom into the victim.

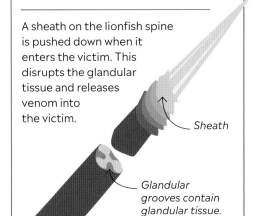

Sheath

Glandular grooves contain glandular tissue.

Lionfish spine

All about rays

Rays are the strange and graceful relatives of sharks, skates, and sawfish. They have winglike fins, cartilage skeletons, and flat bodies that are well adapted to life on the seabed. On the underside of the body are the mouth and gill slits. On top are the eyes and spiracles—openings that draw clean water to the gills. Most rays have flat teeth for grinding shellfish and other bottom-dwelling creatures.

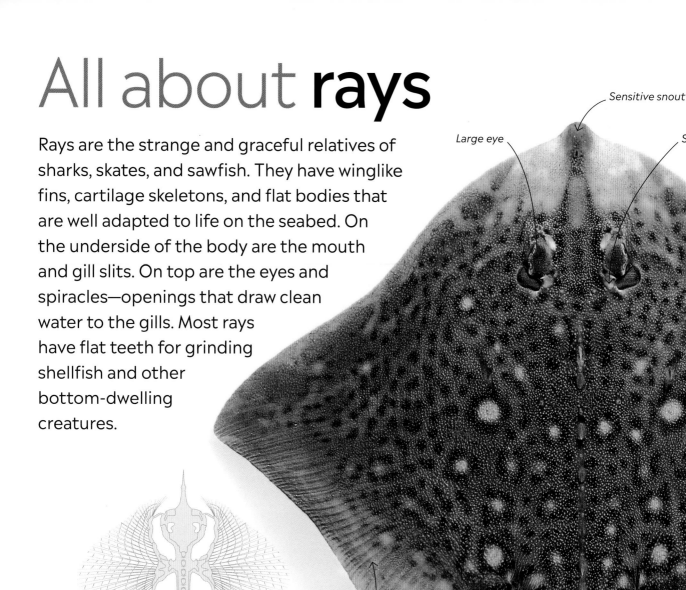

Sensitive snout

Large eye

Spiracle

Back view of female thornback ray

A ray swims by waving its pectoral fins up and down, or in ripples along the edge.

Back is camouflaged to conceal ray on sand.

Flexible fan
The thornback's pectoral fin rays are expanded like a fan, forming a flexible framework for the "wings."

A thornback ray has rows of
sharp thorns
on its back and tail.

Thornback's back
Thornback rays grow to about 3 ft (1 m) and rarely stray to waters deeper than 164 ft (50 m). They feed on crabs and other shellfish, as well as flatfish and sand eels.

Dorsal fin

Buckler thorns along back

Thornback ray in resting pose

Ray at rest
This resting thornback displays the row of sharp thorns, called bucklers, along its back and tail. Its body is slightly arched to allow water to flow through the gill slits underneath.

Buckler thorns along backbone

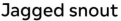

Jagged snout
The sawfish, a member of the ray group, protects itself with its sawlike snout.

Pectoral fins
are joined
to the head.

Nostril

Horny
mouth

Five gill
slits

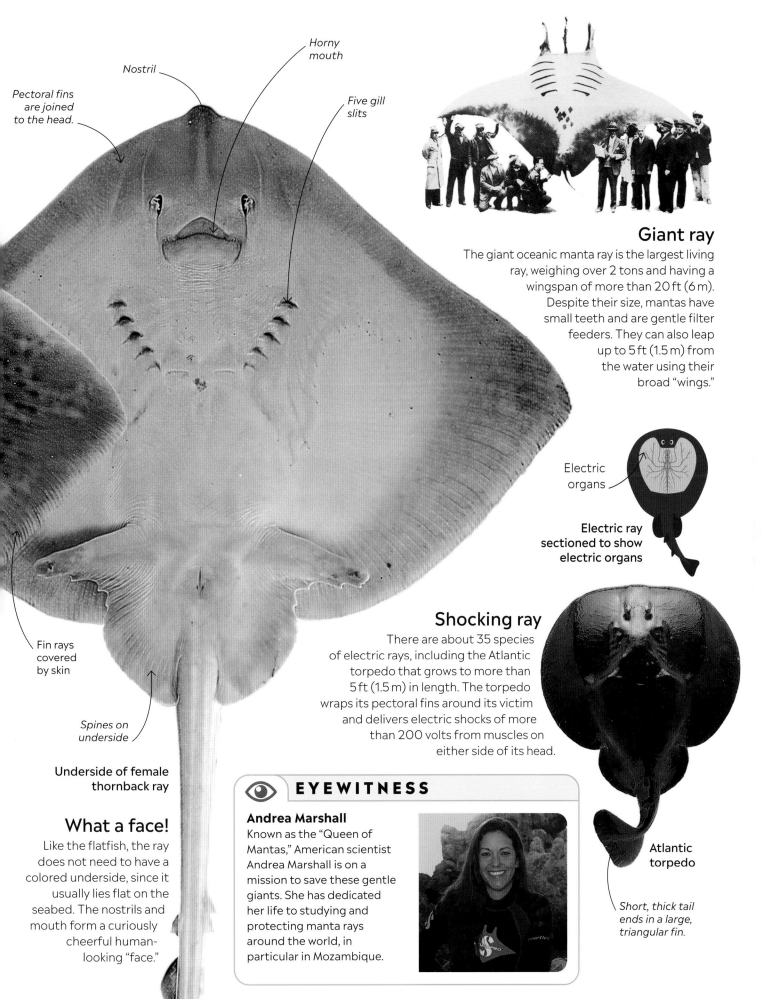

Giant ray

The giant oceanic manta ray is the largest living ray, weighing over 2 tons and having a wingspan of more than 20 ft (6 m). Despite their size, mantas have small teeth and are gentle filter feeders. They can also leap up to 5 ft (1.5 m) from the water using their broad "wings."

Electric organs

Electric ray sectioned to show electric organs

Fin rays covered by skin

Shocking ray

There are about 35 species of electric rays, including the Atlantic torpedo that grows to more than 5 ft (1.5 m) in length. The torpedo wraps its pectoral fins around its victim and delivers electric shocks of more than 200 volts from muscles on either side of its head.

Spines on underside

Underside of female thornback ray

What a face!

Like the flatfish, the ray does not need to have a colored underside, since it usually lies flat on the seabed. The nostrils and mouth form a curiously cheerful human-looking "face."

Atlantic torpedo

Short, thick tail ends in a large, triangular fin.

👁 EYEWITNESS

Andrea Marshall
Known as the "Queen of Mantas," American scientist Andrea Marshall is on a mission to save these gentle giants. She has dedicated her life to studying and protecting manta rays around the world, in particular in Mozambique.

Warriors of the **sea**

Many sharks are powerful and efficient hunters. They charge at prey with sudden speed and bite with bone-crunching power. Yet not all sharks are sleek. The wobbegong, a type of carpet shark, is a slow mover who feeds on bottom-dwelling shellfish, and, like most sharks, it rarely attacks people unless provoked.

Short, blunt snout

Large eyes for hunting

Small, triangular teeth

A shark's gill slits are not covered.

Cladoselache, from 350 million years ago

Frilled shark

The ancient hunter

Sharks have survived largely unchanged for millions of years. An early type of shark was the 6-ft- (2-m-) long *Cladoselache*, which terrorized the seas 350 million years ago. The frilled shark (above) looks more like a primitive species than a modern shark.

 EYEWITNESS

MISS

During the worldwide lockdown in 2020 due to the COVID-19 pandemic, Amani Webber-Schultz, Carlee Jackson, Jaida Elcock, and Jasmin Graham founded Minorities in Shark Science (MISS) in the United States. The group brings together young people of color who study sharks.

Reproduction

Some female sharks lay eggs in the water; others give birth to live young. Most sharks are ovoviviparous—the young develop inside eggs that hatch inside the female's body. The mother gives birth to fully formed baby sharks called pups.

The egg yolk provides energy for the unborn baby shark.

Inside story

Shark skeletons are made of cartilage, not bone. However, the cartilage is not soft and rubbery, but extremely hard—as shown by the power of a shark's bite (p.61). This cat shark skeleton shows the typical shark's heterocercal tail—the upper tail lobe is longer than the lower one.

The vertebral column (backbone) extends into the upper part of the shark's tail.

The skin bears scars of previous hunting encounters.

Typical shark's triangular dorsal fin

Dark gray upper body

Head like a hammer

The eyes and nostrils of the hammerhead shark are set far apart at either side of the "hammer." As the shark swims, it swings its head back and forth searching for stingrays—its favorite prey.

Bump-like second dorsal fin

Film star

The star of the film *Jaws* was a great white shark. These sharks can grow to 21 ft (6.4 m).

White underside

Large pectoral fin

Small pelvic fin

The terrifying motion picture from the terrifying No.1 best seller.

JAWS

ROBERT ... RICHARD ...

Thrashing thresher

The thresher shark uses its remarkable tail to catch prey. It circles a school of smaller fish and sweeps them into a tight group by whipping the water with its tail. It then charges through the school open-mouthed, and snaps up dazed victims. The thresher grows to 20 ft (6 m) but weighs only 1,000 lb (450 kg) as its tail makes up half its overall length.

Continued on next page

Continued from previous page

The warrior's weapons

Sharks never stop growing teeth. In most species the teeth are triangular or pointed, with sharp, serrated edges. If the prey is too big to eat in one bite, the shark will clamp its teeth on the victim's body and shake its head from side-to-side, "sawing" off a mouth-size lump.

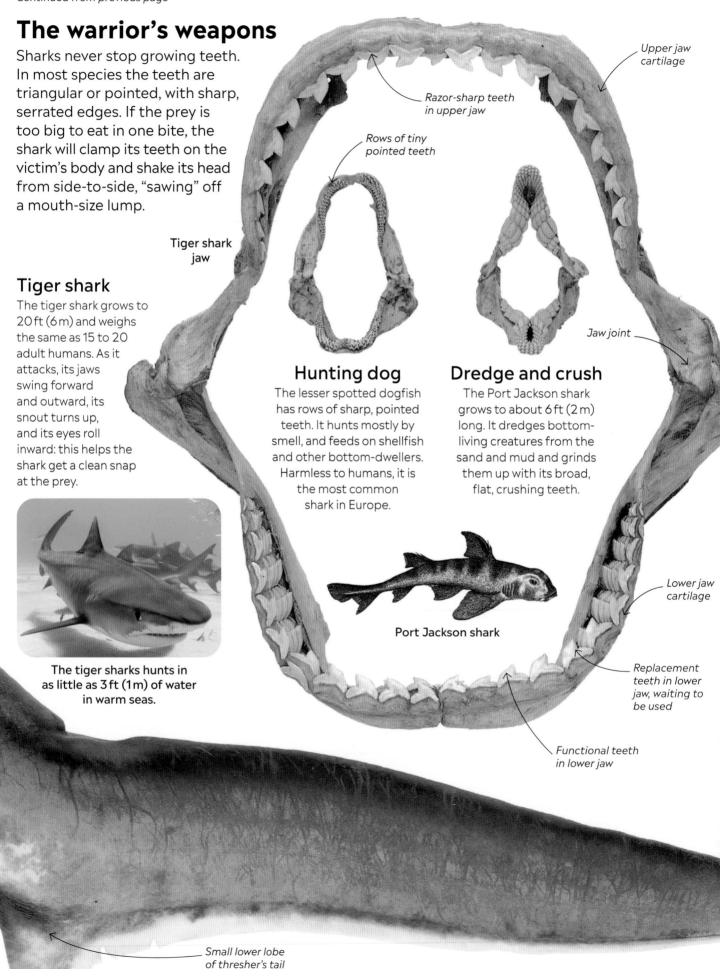

Tiger shark jaw

Razor-sharp teeth in upper jaw

Upper jaw cartilage

Rows of tiny pointed teeth

Jaw joint

Tiger shark

The tiger shark grows to 20 ft (6 m) and weighs the same as 15 to 20 adult humans. As it attacks, its jaws swing forward and outward, its snout turns up, and its eyes roll inward: this helps the shark get a clean snap at the prey.

The tiger sharks hunts in as little as 3 ft (1 m) of water in warm seas.

Hunting dog

The lesser spotted dogfish has rows of sharp, pointed teeth. It hunts mostly by smell, and feeds on shellfish and other bottom-dwellers. Harmless to humans, it is the most common shark in Europe.

Dredge and crush

The Port Jackson shark grows to about 6 ft (2 m) long. It dredges bottom-living creatures from the sand and mud and grinds them up with its broad, flat, crushing teeth.

Port Jackson shark

Lower jaw cartilage

Replacement teeth in lower jaw, waiting to be used

Functional teeth in lower jaw

Small lower lobe of thresher's tail

Biggest has the smallest

The world's biggest shark has some of the smallest teeth. Whale sharks have rows of tooth-shaped denticles (p.14) in their mouth, gills, and throat. These act as a sieve, filtering small creatures from the water as the shark cruises along.

Long upper lobe of thresher's tail

Small teeth made from modified denticles

Rows of whale shark teeth

Basking shark

Basker's teeth

A basking shark (the second largest of all fish) has many small teeth. This huge shark feeds by filtering the water with its gill rakers.

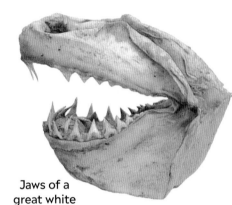

Lower jaw cartilage from basking shark

Thresher's thrash

The thresher's tail is extremely muscular, tough, and strong, and can be flexed (bent) at will. The tail hits fish and creates a stunning shock wave in the water.

Great white shark

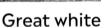

Great white

The great white is the most powerful of all sharks. A big shark can exert a force of 132 lb (60 kg) through just one tooth!

Jaws of a great white

Exposed teeth ready for use

Teeth developing within jaw

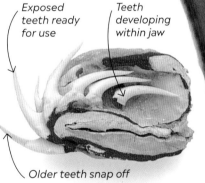

Older teeth snap off

New teeth

Sharks continuously grow new teeth at the back of the jaws. These gradually move forward until they reach the front. As the working teeth break off, new ones from behind take their place.

Sense of smell

Sharks get a heightened sense of smell from the sensitive olfactory lamellae (membranes) inside their nostrils. Up to two-thirds of the total weight of a shark's brain is dedicated to processing smells.

The tail can swipe through 180° in one-third of a second.

Studying **fish**

In laboratories around the world, fish are studied by specialists called ichthyologists. Fish populations are constantly monitored to determine whether certain species are in danger, or whether overfished species are regaining their numbers.

See-through staining

Fish bodies are studied using various chemicals. Here, the creature's soft organs are turned to a transparent jelly. The harder parts, such as the bones, are stained pink. The complete skeleton can then be examined under the microscope.

X-ray fish

Fish bones and cartilage show up white on an X-ray. Such images can be used to investigate fish diseases.

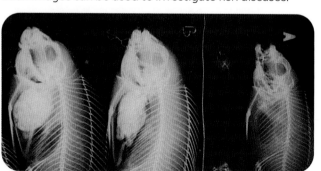

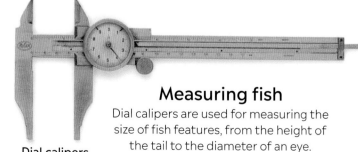

Dial calipers

Measuring fish

Dial calipers are used for measuring the size of fish features, from the height of the tail to the diameter of an eye.

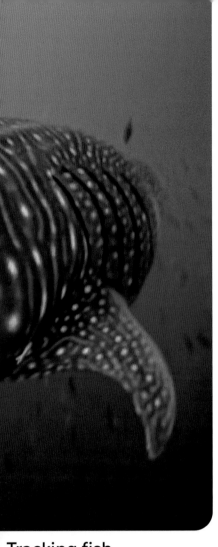

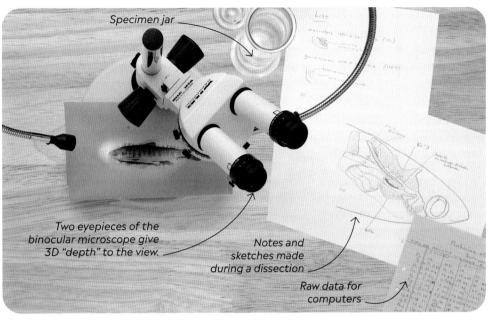

Specimen jar

Two eyepieces of the binocular microscope give 3D "depth" to the view.

Notes and sketches made during a dissection

Raw data for computers

Studying a specimen

Fish specimens are stored in alcohol to preserve them. As ichthyologists work on a fish, they make notes and draw sketches. A diagram is usually easier to understand than a written description. A binocular microscope (above) reveals parts that are too small for the naked eye to see. A scanning electron microscope shows details at more than 10,000 times life-size.

Tracking fish

Whale sharks go on long migrations across the ocean basins. Scuba diving scientists attach satellite tags to their dorsal fins to track their journeys, measuring their location, speed, and depth.

Bone chisel for cutting through tough scutes and bone

Scalpel for cutting nerves

Fine scalpel

Scalpel

Syringe for injecting preservatives into fish

Tools for the job

Various tools are used to examine a fish's body. It requires great skill to expose the organs without damaging them.

Angled probe for parting tissue

Forceps for lifting out various vessels

176   Color Illustrations

Rainbow trout *Salmo gairdneri*

Brook trout *Salvelinus fontinalis*

Fish gallery

Reference books and catalogs help identify new or unfamiliar specimens.

Did you know?

FASCINATING FACTS

Koi fish often outlive their original owners and are handed down to the next generation. Although the average lifespan of a koi is 40 to 60 years, one koi in Japan was reported to be 230 years old!

An anglerfish has an enormous, toothy mouth. It is capable of eating almost anything. Anglerfish can even swallow other fish that are equal to their own weight.

Don't put your money on a seahorse. They are one of the slowest swimmers in the sea.

The fairy basslet fish can change gender at will. If there are no males around to mate with, the female fairy basslet fish changes into a male.

Dorsal fin

Seahorse

Tame koi fish can be fed by hand.

Puffer fish can puff up with water when in danger, but what they really like to fill up on is food!

A juvenile orbicular batfish plays dead when danger is near. It floats motionless on its side, resembling a dead leaf floating on the surface of the water.

A fish fry is not just something to enjoy with french fries. It is also the name for a baby fish.

Flashlight fish give off a strange green glow to help them see in the dark. The light is generated by bacteria living in special pouches under the fish's eyes.

The candiru is a tiny fish with a nearly transparent body. This scary fish from South America has a vampire's thirst for blood, human or animal.

Anableps (four-eyed fish) can see above and below water at the same time—very handy for finding food.

Rains of fish have been documented for thousands of years. When waterspouts (tornadoes that form over water) pass over water, they pick up fish and carry them into the clouds. When the clouds open later and rain begins to fall, so do the fish. Roman writer Pliny the Younger described a fishy rain in the 1st century CE.

Fish cluster near coral tentacles for protection.

Coral reef

Coral's hard skeleton is secreted by marine creatures.

QUESTIONS AND ANSWERS

What is the largest fish?

The enormous whale shark has been recorded at 65 ft (20 m) long. Its mouth alone is 4 ft (1.2 m) wide! This supersize fish eats vast numbers of plankton that pass through its toothy grin.

Which is the longest-lived fish?

A Greenland shark has been estimated to be about 400 years old. These sharks grow slowly at just ⅓ in (1 cm) a year. They live in the freezing cold waters of the Arctic Ocean and swim slowly, which helps them save energy in the cold.

Do fish sleep?

That depends on how you define sleep. Fish do not share the brain wave changes of human sleep, but they do have sleeplike periods, lowered response to stimuli, and slower physical activity. Some fish, such as the parrotfish, blow out a large bubble of mucus to make a cocoon and sleep in it!

Do flying fish really fly?

No. They jump out of the water and glide, using their lower tail lobe to help them move. "Flights" of more than 300 ft (90 m) have been known, but a typical glide distance is much shorter.

What is the smallest deep-sea fish?

At only ⅛ in (6.2 mm) long, the male *Photocorynus spiniceps* is one of the smallest deep-sea fish.

Photocorynus spiniceps male

How fast can fish swim?

The sailfish is the fastest thing on fins. This fish has been measured at speeds of up to 68 mph (109 kph). That's as fast as a cheetah!

How far can a fish swim?

Pacific bluefin tuna have been tracked swimming up to 25,000 miles (40,230 km) from Japan to California and back.

Which fish lays the most eggs?

The ocean sunfish has a round, flat body like a giant, gray stone wheel. It lays an incredible 30 million eggs in one spawning, making it by far the most fertile in the fish world.

FREAKY FISH STORIES

Fish have been around for some 500 million years, but they're still making news. Here are the true tales of some extremely odd fish.

➤ In the 2003 movie *Finding Nemo*, a fish is flushed down the toilet to return to the sea. After hundreds of children set their fish "free" in this way, the film studio had to launch a "Don't Flush the Fish" campaign.

➤ In 2004, a man accidentally dropped his phone into an aquarium. A huge catfish promptly ate it in one bite. The man's attempts to call his own cell phone number to see which fish vibrated did not work.

➤ In 2004, a Norwegian fisherman was stunned when a codfish he hauled in with his daily catch contained an intact, unopened cola can.

Which is the most ferocious predatory fish in fresh water?

That would be the legendary South African piranha. This river fish has a mouthful of sharp, triangular teeth that chop through prey in minutes.

Piranha

Which is the largest predatory ocean fish?

With 3,000 teeth, the great white shark is the ocean's largest and most feared fish predator. These 20-ft- (6-m-) long creatures prowl the world's subtropical waters.

Mouthful of teeth

Triangular fins

White underside helps the shark "disappear" from below.

Great white shark

Do fish hear?

Yes, but hearing abilities vary by species. A fish hears as sensory chambers in its inner ear detect differences in sound vibrations. In some fish, the swim bladder plays a role in transmitting these vibrations. If you tap on the glass of an aquarium, a fish will "hear" it as pressure against the side of its body.

Fish tales

Fish have always been important to human cultures, so it's no surprise that these fascinating finned creatures have appeared in so many myths and legends. Here are a few of those fishy fables.

GODS AND HEROES

In many myths, gods and heroes appear in the form of fish. In some, the gods are half-human and half-fish. In others, gods change into fish for protection. Fish are often associated with life and creation.

What a catch!
Mythological figure Maui appears in many myths from the Polynesian Islands and New Zealand, as a god in some stories and a mortal hero in others. New Zealand legend tells of the hero Maui who cast a magic fish hook. When Maui and his brothers pulled the fishing line, they raised the North Island of New Zealand out of the waters.

School of fish
The Mesopotamian god Oannes brought wisdom to humans. With a man's head on a fish's body, he rose from the seabed each day to teach science and art.

The ones that got away
In Roman mythology, the gods Venus and Cupid were out walking one day when they met the giant, Typhon. Terrified, they jumped into the river and took the form of fish. The other gods lifted the fish to the sky to form the constellation Pisces.

Triton calling
Half man, half fish, the Greek god Triton is often depicted holding a conch shell. He could raise or lower the ocean waves with a single call from his shell.

Triton statue and fountain

FISH AND RELIGION

The fish is one of the earliest symbols in many religions. In Judaism, a fish is considered a symbol of fertility and luck. In Christianity, it represents both Jesus Christ and his believers.

Loaves and fishes
In one of the miracles of the Bible, Jesus feeds a crowd of 5,000 people with just five loaves of bread and two fish.

Tile mosaic of the loaves and fishes

New Year blessings
Fish is a traditional food eaten during the Jewish New Year as it represents good fortune for the new year.

Flood warning
One of the three supreme deities in Hinduism, God Vishnu appeared to humans in 10 avatars (incarnations) to provide help. In his first avatar, he took the form of a fish to warn of a flood.

The fish symbol used by Christians since the first century may have a pagan origin.

Christian symbol
In Christianity, the fish is a symbol for Christ. This may be because in Greek, the first letters of the words "Jesus Christ Son of God" spell *Ichthus*, or fish.

MONSTERS OF THE DEEP

Although sea creatures in mythology were usually harmless, there were some who were downright monstrous.

Hippocampus
This creature is a sea animal from Greek mythology. Its head resembles a horse, and its hind parts a fish. Poseidon, the god of the sea, hitches the Hippocampus to his chariot to pull it across the waves. This is why the scientific (genus) name for seahorses is *Hippocampus*.

Call of the mermaid
Mermaids and sirens appear in many myths. The mermaid has the body of a woman and the tail of a fish. A siren may also appear as half-female, half-fish. Her singing has the power to lure men to their deaths.

Mermaid statue in Copenhagen, Denmark

Nixes
Norse folklore tells of nixes—water spirits in fish or human form that lure people into the water to drown. There is one way to spot a nix in human form: the hems of its clothes are wet.

Poison arrows
In Pacific Island legends, there are some pretty fishy characters. The adaro, for example, is a nasty sea-spirit who is half-human, half-fish. He rides across the waves on rainbows, killing people by shooting poisonous fish at them.

Sideshow hoax
In 1842, legendary showman P. T. Barnum exhibited the remains of a "Mermaid from Fiji" in his museum. But this was a hoax—the mermaid was a monkey's head stitched onto a fish's tail!

Engraving of fishy sea monsters lurking in the waters

Scary sea creatures
In the 1400s, when Europeans started sailing across oceans to explore the world, they knew little of what lurked in the waters. Sailors were scared of being gobbled by gigantic sea monsters after a shipwreck. This engraving shows various sea beasts to watch out for.

FISH AS SYMBOLS

From representations of wealth to signs of the zodiac, fish appear as symbols throughout the world. In many cultures, they are considered to be a source of wisdom and power.

The sign of the fish
As early as 3000 BCE, ancient Mesopotamian scholars recorded the signs of the zodiac we know today. The pair of fish, called Pisces, represent the star constellation of the same name.

Good luck fish
In Japan, the tai fish is considered a symbol of good luck. In spring, these fish take on a reddish color. Because red is also a lucky color, tai are especially prized at that time.

Fishing for wealth
For thousands of years, the carp has been a symbol of wealth and power in China. Many people display an image of a golden carp in their homes.

Symbolic salmon
The salmon is an important symbol among Indigenous peoples of the US Pacific Northwest coast. Because it swims so determinedly upstream to find its birthplace, it represents courage and perseverance.

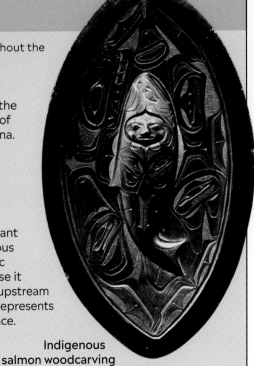

Indigenous salmon woodcarving

Find out more

There's a whole world of fish to discover—here's how to dive in! An excellent place to begin is an aquarium, where you'll find exhibits of all kinds of fish species. A visit to a natural history museum will provide information on modern and prehistoric fish. You could also visit a theme park, or buy an aquarium to create your own small-scale aquatic community.

A tunnel of fish

Many aquariums feature freshwater fish, marine fish, and a host of other sea creatures to help you understand and explore fish habitats. The Audubon Aquarium of the Americas in New Orleans features a crystal-clear tunnel (left) that gives aquarium visitors the experience of being surrounded on three sides by water—and fish.

The fish uses its large mouth to gulp plenty of plankton.

Paddlefish

Visitors to the Tennessee Aquarium can learn about this unusual paddlefish from the Mississippi River. Its paddle is covered in taste buds that help it find plankton as it cruises the river.

Hands-on learning

Many aquatic parks feature tide pool exhibits and small tanks that allow you to touch specimens. These visitors to the Monterey Bay Aquarium in California are reaching out to touch sealife.

USEFUL WEBSITES

- Explore the ocean realm with the National Oceanic and Atmospheric Administration: **http://oceanexplorer.noaa.gov**
- The home site of the Monterey Bay Aquarium Research Institute: **www.mbari.org**
- Dive deep into the lives of fish with the Australian Museum: **https://australian.museum/learn/animals/fishes/**
- Learn more about how to protect the ocean with the UK's Marine Conservation Society: **https://www.mcsuk.org/**

Fish on film

Movies such as *Shark Tale* bring the undersea world to life through amazing computer animation. These movies illustrate the fascination that marine life continues to hold.

A window to the world of fish

A fish tank is a great way to observe a habitat on a small scale. You can buy starter sets that contain everything you need at most pet stores. Try to select fish species that were bred in captivity, and not taken from the wild. Remember that fish are living creatures that need care and attention.

Rocks and plants create a lifelike habitat.

PLACES TO VISIT

MONTEREY BAY AQUARIUM, MONTEREY, CA
This award-winning aquarium contains more than 200 exhibits.

NATIONAL AQUARIUM, WASHINGTON, D.C.
America's oldest aquarium, this national treasure features more than 80 exhibits with 2,000 freshwater and marine species.

NATIONAL AQUARIUM, PLYMOUTH, UK
The largest aquarium in the UK, it contains more than 4,000 animals.

VANCOUVER AQUARIUM, VANCOUVER, CANADA
Canada's largest aquarium features 8,000 animals and an Arctic Habitat exhibit.

OSAKA AQUARIUM KAIYUKAN, OSAKA, JAPAN
When it opened in 1990, this was the world's largest aquarium.

DUBAI AQUARIUM AND UNDERWATER ZOO, DUBAI, UAE
Located in the Dubai Mall, it includes more than 400 sharks and rays in a 10-million-gallon tank.

Fish have gills, but you'll need a tank.

Down time

Scuba diving is as close as you are going to get to being a fish yourself! Divers usually need to complete a 20-hour certification course run by one of the sport's major organizations.

Glossary

A shark's dorsal fin helps it steer and stop.

Shark in profile

AQUATIC Growing or living, or taking place, in or upon water.

BARBEL One of the fleshy, touch-sensitive whiskers on fish, such as catfish.

BREACHING When a whale, or shark, leaps clear out of the ocean water.

BUOYANCY The tendency or ability to float or rise in liquid or air.

CAMOUFLAGE A way an animal conceals itself, for example, from a predator.

CARTILAGINOUS Having a skeleton made up mostly of cartilage (tough, elastic tissue).

CAUDAL At or near the tail.

CICHLID Any of a family of tropical and subtropical freshwater fish, similar to sunfish.

COCOON A protective cover in which an immature animal shelters itself.

CYCLOID Having fish scales that are rounded in form with smooth edges.

DENTICLE A small tooth, or a toothlike projection.

DORSAL Of or on the back.

EEL Any of a large variety of fish with long, slippery snakelike bodies and no pelvic fin.

EGG CASE Protective sac where an embryo grows.

LARVAL Of the immature form of an animal before it reaches adulthood.

LATERAL LINE A row of sensory organs along each side of the body of a fish, probably used to detect currents, vibrations, and pressure changes.

LOBE A rounded, projecting part of the body.

MAMMAL A warm-blooded vertebrate.

MEMBRANE A thin, soft sheet of animal tissue, serving as a covering or lining for an organ or for a body part.

MERMAID'S PURSE Nickname for the dried-out egg cases of certain fish that wash up on the beach.

METAMORPHOSIS In biology, a change in form, structure, or function as a result of development.

MOUTHBREEDER A fish that cares for its eggs and young in its mouth.

MUCUS A thick, slimy substance that moistens and protects membranes.

OPERCULUM The bony covering protecting the gills of fish.

PARASITE A plant or animal that lives on or in an organism from a different species.

PECTORAL FIN One of a pair of fins just behind the head of a fish.

PELVIC FIN One of a pair of fins at the pelvic girdle of a fish.

Caudal fin

COELACANTH A primitive fish (dating back some 400 million years).

CORAL The hard rocklike skeleton secreted by certain marine polyps and deposited in extensive masses.

CORAL REEF A ridge built mostly of coral in shallow, tropical seas.

COUNTERSHADING Animal coloring with a darker back and paler belly.

CRUSTACEAN An animal with a hard outer shell that usually lives in water.

CTENOID Having an edge with projections like the teeth of a comb.

EMBRYO An animal in the earliest stages of its development.

EXOSKELETON Any hard, secreted external supporting structure, like an oyster's shell.

FERTILIZE In biology, to impregnate or pollinate and make fruitful.

FIN Any of several winglike, membranous bodies on a fish, used in swimming, turning, and balancing.

FISH Any of a large group of cold-blooded vertebrate animals living in water; fish have gills for breathing, fins, and usually scales.

GANOID Of a group of primitive fish covered by rows of hard, glossy enameled scales or plates.

GILL The breathing organ for most animals that live in water.

ICHTHYOLOGY The branch of zoology dealing with fish.

Egg case

PLACOID Having horny scales with a toothlike spine.

PREDATOR One who captures and feeds on other animals.

PREHENSILE Adapted for grasping by wrapping or folding around something.

PROPULSION Something that pushes or drives an object forward.

SCALE Any of the thin, flat, overlapping plates forming the outer covering of a fish.

Scales

SCHOOL A large number of fish of the same kind swimming together in unison.

SCUTE Any external bony or horny plate.

SHELLFISH Any aquatic animal with a shell such as a lobster.

SPAWNING Producing or depositing eggs or young.

SPECIES In biology, a classification of plants or animals; members of a species have a high degree of similarity and can usually breed only among themselves.

SPINE A sharp, stiff projection on the body of certain animals.

SPIRACLE A circular opening for air or respiratory water.

STREAMLINING A way of contouring that offers the least resistance when moving through water or air.

SWIM BLADDER A gas-filled sac in most fish which gives the body buoyancy.

TELEOST A member of a large group of bony fish with a symmetrical tail fin and a swim bladder.

TENTACLE Any of a variety of long, slender growths around the head and mouth.

TRANSVERSE LINE A crosswise line; on a fish, the transverse line runs from back to belly.

TROPICAL Of the region on Earth between the Tropic of Cancer and the Tropic of Capricorn.

VENOMOUS Containing, or full of, venom; poisonous.

Ray's fins contain visible spines

Female thornback ray

VIVIPAROUS Bearing live young (as most mammals do) instead of laying eggs.

WHALE A large, warm-blooded, fishlike mammal that breathes air, bears live young, and has a flat, horizontal tail.

YAW To swing on the vertical axis; for example, as a fish swims.

YOLK SAC In zoology, the saclike membrane containing yolk that nourishes an embryo.

Yellow seahorse

Tubelike mouth

Prehensile tail

Index

Acknowledgments

The publisher would like to thank the following people with their help with making the book:
Geoff Potts, Fred Frettsome, and Vicky Irlam at the Marine Biological Association, Plymouth; Rick Elliot, and the staff at Waterlife Research Industries Ltd; Neil Fletcher, Simon Newnes & Partners, Billingsgate, London; Richard Davies of OSF for photography on pp. 28–29, 23–33; Bari Howell at MAFF, Conwy for supplying eggs and hatchings on pp. 24–25; Barney Kindersley; Lester Cheeseman and Jane Coney for additional design work; John Woodcock for illustrations; Kathy Lockley for picture research; Dr. Amanda Vincent for editorial advice; Aman Kumar for editorial assistance; Shanker Prasad and Dheeraj Singh for DTP assistance; Jo Penning for the index; and Ann Baggaley and Hazel Beynon for proofreading.

The publisher would like to thank the following for their kind permission to reproduce their images:
(Key: a-above; b-below/bottom; c-center; f-far; l-left; r-right; t-top)

3 Getty Images: Wild Horizon / Universal Images Group (bl). **naturepl.com:** Georgette Douwma (cb). **7 Dreamstime.com:** Centrill (tr). Getty Images: Colin McConnell / Toronto Star (bc). **8 naturepl.com:** Alex Mustard (r). **12–13 Science Photo Library:** Peter Scoones (bc). **13 McGregor Museum:** Kimberley (cla). **14 Science Photo Library:** Ted Kinsman (bl). **17 Getty Images:** Wild Horizon / Universal Images Group (cr). **18 Philip Dowell:** (tl), (clb), (cbr). **18–19 naturepl.com:** David Shale (bl). **20–21 Alamy Stock Photo:** J M Barres / Agefotostock (c). **20 naturepl.com:** Tony Wu (br). **21 Getty Images:** Alex Wong (br). **naturepl. com:** Georgette Douwma (bl). **22 Getty Images:** Chris Conner / Eyeem (r). **naturepl.com:** Tony Wu (clb). **23 Dreamstime.com:** Zepherwind (bl). **Shutterstock.com:** Nick Harvey (cb/Heather Koldewey). **Amanda Vincent, Project Seahorse:** Andaya Vincent (cb). **27 Dave King:** (br). **28 Getty Images / iStock:** Alessandro De Maddalena (tl). **28–29 naturepl.com:** Andy Murch (c). **29 SuperStock:** Flip Nicklin / Minden Pictures (tl), **Mary Evans Picture Library:** Robert Harding Picture Library (br); **Daniel Quinn and Qiang Zhong:** Yicong Fu, University of Virginia (cl). **30 Alamy Stock Photo:** Rodrigo Friscione / Cultura Creative RF (cl). **naturepl.com:** Sue Daly (ca). **32 Alamy Stock Photo:** Sue Daly / Nature Picture Library (tl). **33 naturepl.com:** Daniel Heuclin (tl). **Georgia Institute of Technology:** Rob Felt and Daniel Goldman (cra). **34 Alamy Stock Photo:** Mr Paulo Oliveira (r). **35 Getty Images:** Lynn Pelham (bl). **37 Ardea:** (br). **38–39 Dorling Kindersley:** Dreamstime.com: Mohamed Osama (c). **40–41 naturepl.com:** Nature Production (ca). **41 naturepl. com:** Nature Production (ca). **42 Getty Images:** San Francisco Chronicle / Hearst Newspapers (cb). **43 Getty Images:** Oxford Scientific / Photodisc (cla). **Shutterstock.com:** Studio KIWI (br). **44–45 Shutterstock.com:** Radek Borovka (b). **44 Dreamstime.com:** Jaap Bleijenberg (cl). **Getty Images / iStock:** Wrangel (tl). **45 Alamy Stock Photo:** Aqua Press / Biosphoto (c). **46–47 naturepl.com:** Georgette Douwma (c). **46 Alamy Stock Photo:** WaterFrame_mza (tl). **47 Alamy Stock Photo:** Cbimages (tr). **49 John & Gillian Lythgoe:** (cra). **51 naturepl.com:** Alex Mustard (tr). **52–53 Alamy Stock Photo:** Franco Banfi / Nature Picture Library (b). **53 Alamy Stock Photo:** Blue Planet Archive MVA (cra). **54 Getty Images / iStock:** Shakzu (cla). **Frank Spooner Pictures:** (bc), (bl). **54–55 Getty Images:** Emma Holman / Moment (c). **55 Getty Images:** Cigdem Uzun (tr). **57 QUEEN OF MANTAS:** Dr. Andrea Marshall (bc). **58 Minorities in Shark Sciences (MISS):** Cliff Hawkins (bl). **59:** Kobal Collection (bl). **60 Dreamstime.com:** Naluphoto (clb). **61 Alamy Stock Photo:** © John Pendygraft / Tampa Bay Times via ZUMA Press Wire Service (br). **Dreamstime.com:** William Lowe (crb). **62–63 Galápagos Whale Shark Project:** © Jenny Waack (tl). **62 David Morbey/ Natural History Museum:** (bl). **63 Dreamstime.com:** HAKINMHAN (tr). **64 Alamy Stock Photo:** WaterFrame_dpr (b). **Getty Images / iStock:** Olga_Anourina (tc). **65 Alamy Stock Photo:** Reinhard Dirscherl (tl). **Dorling Kindersley: Dreamstime.com:** Nerthuz (cr). **Getty Images / iStock:** F9photos (cra). **66 Alamy Stock Photo:** Prisma Archivo (bl). **Dreamstime.com:** Viktor Onyshchenko (cra). **67 AKG-Images:** (tr); **Dorling Kindersley:** (bl); **Demetrio Carrasco:** (cl); **Seattle Art Museum, Gift of John H. Hauberg:** (br). **68 Alamy Stock Photo:** David R. Frazier Photolibrary, Inc. (crb); **Audubon Nature Institute:** David Bull (cl); **Tennessee Aquarium:** Richard T. Bryant (bl); Todd Stanley (tl). **69 Alamy Stock Photo:** PictureLux / The Hollywood Archive (tc); Travelscape Images (b). **Dorling Kindersley:** Paul Bricknell (c). **70 Frank Greenaway:** (t); **Kim Taylor:** (br); **Jerry Young:** (bl). **71 Alamy Stock Photo:** Alex Mustard / Nature Picture Library (b); **Dave King:** (cr); **Jerry Young:** (tr); **Dorling Kindersley:** Jane Burton (b).

All other images © Dorling Kindersley

For further information see:
www.dkimages.com

WHAT WILL YOU EYEWITNESS NEXT?

Packed with pictures and full of facts, DK Eyewitness books are perfect for school projects and home learning.

AMERICAN REVOLUTION

ANCIENT EGYPT

ANCIENT ROME

CAT

CLIMATE CHANGE

DINOSAUR

FISH

HURRICANE & TORNADO

NATURAL DISASTERS

OCEAN

ROCKS & MINERALS

SHARK

THE AMAZON

THE ELEMENTS

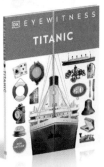
TITANIC

TRAIN

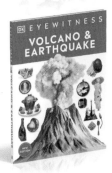
VOLCANO & EARTHQUAKE

WEATHER

WONDERS OF THE WORLD

WORLD WAR II

Also available:

Eyewitness Amphibian
Eyewitness Ancient China
Eyewitness Ancient Civilizations
Eyewitness Ancient Greece
Eyewitness Animal
Eyewitness Arms and Armor
Eyewitness Astronomy
Eyewitness Aztec, Inca & Maya
Eyewitness Baseball
Eyewitness Bible Lands
Eyewitness Bird
Eyewitness Car
Eyewitness Castle

Eyewitness Chemistry
Eyewitness Crystals & Gems
Eyewitness Dog
Eyewitness Early People
Eyewitness Eagle and Birds of Prey
Eyewitness Electricity
Eyewitness Endangered Animals
Eyewitness Energy
Eyewitness Flight
Eyewitness Forensic Science
Eyewitness Fossil
Eyewitness Great Scientists
Eyewitness Horse

Eyewitness Human Body
Eyewitness Insect
Eyewitness Judaism
Eyewitness Knight
Eyewitness Medieval Life
Eyewitness Mesopotamia
Eyewitness Money
Eyewitness Mummy
Eyewitness Mythology
Eyewitness National Parks
Eyewitness North American Indian
Eyewitness Plant
Eyewitness Planets
Eyewitness Prehistoric Life

Eyewitness Presidents
Eyewitness Religion
Eyewitness Reptile
Eyewitness Robot
Eyewitness Shakespeare
Eyewitness Soccer
Eyewitness Soldier
Eyewitness Space Exploration
Eyewitness The Civil War
Eyewitness Tree
Eyewitness Universe
Eyewitness Vietnam War
Eyewitness Viking
Eyewitness World War I

DK For the curious